BEST
NEW
POETS
2012

BEST
NEW
POETS
2012

MATTHEW DICKMAN
GUEST EDITOR

JAZZY DANZIGER
SERIES EDITOR

This book was published in cooperation with *Meridian*, readmeridian.org, and Samovar Press.

For additional information on *Best New Poets*, visit us at
bestnewpoets.org
twitter.com/BestNewPoets
facebook.com/BestNewPoets

Cover illustration by Dan Zettwoch
danzettwoch.com

Text set in Adobe Garamond Pro and Big Caslon

Printed by Thomson-Shore, Dexter, Michigan

ISBN 13: 978-0-9766296-7-2
ISSN 1554-7019

Contents

About Best New Poets

Welcome to *Best New Poets 2012*, our eighth installment of fifty poems from emerging writers. In *Best New Poets*, the term "emerging writer" is defined as someone who has yet to publish a book-length collection of poetry. The goal of *Best New Poets* is to provide special encouragement and recognition to new poets, the many writing programs they attend, and the magazines that publish their work.

From February to April of 2012, *Best New Poets* accepted nominations from writing programs and magazines in the United States and Canada. Each magazine and program could nominate two writers, each of whom would be granted a free submission. For a small reading fee, writers who had not received nominations could submit two poems as part of our Open Competition, which ran from April 5 to May 25. Eligible poems were either unpublished or published after April 15, 2011.

In all, we received 1715 submissions for a total of roughly 3400 poems. Six readers and the series editor blindly ranked these submissions, sending a few hundred selections to this year's guest editor, Matthew Dickman, who chose the final fifty poems.

To learn more, visit us online at bestnewpoets.org, or follow us on Twitter (@BestNewPoets) or Facebook (facebook.com/BestNewPoets).

Introduction

Anthologies, even yearly anthologies like *Best New Poets*, are funny creatures. They can feel like islands, a kind of complete ecosystem of chosen writers. And because some writers have been chosen we know that others have been voted off the palm-tree-and-white-sand beaches. This can incite a kind of emotional mutiny within the tribe of writers and readers. Dana Gioia touches on this when he writes, "It is a truth universally acknowledged—at least it should be—that an anthology is a book that omits your favorite poem" while Thom Gunn has said, "The institution of the anthology...is at best a convenience for teachers but otherwise a pernicious modern nuisance which keeps readers away from books of poetry."

But I like to think of anthologies more like a party. Anthologies are a kind of malleable gathering that will change depending on whether the hootenanny is on a Friday or a Saturday and who's available, who's bringing the beer and who's bringing the onion dip. It's a celebration of a moment, an idea, in fact a passing idea, of what's going on out in the literary dark. Reading through the box of poems that arrived at my small apartment in Southeast Portland reminded me of one of the great inner organs of art: empathy. Much of what I spent my nights reading were poems that were both written from the life of the poet as well as reaching out toward the celebration of the other, whether that manifested itself in the form of a person, of love, of the night sky, or pure mystery. In all the poems there was an energetic mind looking for meaning. And after all, isn't the search for meaning one of our great adventures as human beings? The poems also reminded me that no one should ever worry about "the state of poetry" for with every new poem, and with every new poet, there is another key quickly unlocking the dark space of imagination and illuminating our lives with the light found just beyond that door.

—Matthew Dickman
August 2012
Portland, Oregon

*The series editor wishes to
acknowledge:*

Jeb Livingood

Lisa Fink

Cecilia Llompart

Guion Pratt

Marielle Prince

Jocelyn Sears

Gina Wohlsdorf

Sean Bishop

Black Hole Owners Association

Hello. And welcome to One-of-Us,
        however you came to be. Maybe one trailed you
            to the highway's charitable din, when,
                lost at dusk in a Texan swamp, you discovered it
                    like a marvelous and terrifying orchid.
Maybe you're a boy with a bucket of pond water
or alternately a grown man honestly in love,
        and you've learned at last that your tadpole is a minnow
        or the woman in question will never grow to love you,
            causing a grain-sized singularity to pearl itself
            at the center of your disappointment.
It could be that you are very very ill
        and there it was one day, a pill among the others;
or someone died—maybe it was discovered
        at the scattering: a marble in the empty urn.

Whatever the cause, though: welcome, welcome.
        There are things we feel you need to know:
You should name it, of course, but please don't name it
        Regret or Oblivion or Sadness or Hurt
        From Which I Suspect I Will Never Recover.
            "Oh Sadness," you might say, "come lie
                with me in bed for an hour
                while the moon takes off its dress."

Or: "Oh Oblivion, you've made such an awful mess
of things again."
You shouldn't encourage it. You shouldn't feed it,
either, though it will seem to ask to be fed,
bending the space around its bowl—

Don't give it a bowl. Don't get too close. Your black hole
is going to take a lot of time; time will nearly stop,
in fact, in its vicinity. You will sleep for days
without knowing. Your minutes
will be your neighbors' hours.
"What did you do this week?,"
your friends will ask, and you will say
you ate breakfast
or bought a t-shirt at the mall
or sampled that new quadruple flavor-changing gum
while their lives will seem an impossible bustle
of joy and actual achievements.

Like a tortoise, your black hole will outlive you.
You will pass it on. Already
you should think of your small patch of darkness
as the darkness of your children. Late into the night and alone,
they will run their grownup hands along its outer regions
and be reminded of you.
Take comfort in that—though you are right to feel pity.
Your black hole, after all, is a sort of hell
that sulks in the corner and churns and churns
and renders all the nightlights useless when,
groggy and dream-spooked, your children rise from bed to pee.

We're sorry that by necessity we will never meet you.
On one of your walks, should you see another walker
      with an impossible dimple of emptiness straining against its chain,
      feel free to wave but please do not approach—

all tooth and gullet and terrible maw,
      you have no idea what they would do to one another.

Sophia G. Starmack

Alice Considers History

if I too / thinks Alice / then the glacier / in the beginning grinding its fingers / the grit of schist and granite / sticks to its lonely bone / its white soul to steer it / a whalebone whistling north if the glacier / thinks Alice / then I / if I too then the ice / if I too / then the mouth / of the river the mouths / of the dead through my dream if I / too then the rock and the names / carved in the rock if I / too then my mother / her fringed leather jacket / if I too then the calf / and the cow's hanging udder if / I too then the field and / each wheatspear turning if I / too then the song / under the lightshafts striking / if I too then each / blade of sun unturning / and the darkness and / the darkness hollering / over the valley and / after ten millennia / even a glacier / gives up the ghost

Lexa Hillyer

Lyrics to the Radiator's Hymn

Ice crackles, loses itself
      in whiskey. So just go…go now
            on your glass wings—

The night's lung heaves, a skyline glazed
in freezing light constricting:
      pink and soft somewhere.

      Heat's whisper.
         The more I call, the more you take form
          cloud-like before me.

Starlings pump through the streets, the city's
            subveins: suddenly
               dark-flown,
        forming a lost, past-less monster.

But we've known the story all along. And it isn't nice:

      preserved in the arched branch
           of the mind, the old ice box…
              frost-flung.

   It was a quality you once adored: how we held
      whole myths in our elegant throats.

Made of something hard,
we crack, blown round from deep within the walls
                    and spurt, froth, wail—

            Oh we coveted

                    but we didn't dare.

        And like moths, the cold always wants in.
Desperate condensation, terrible jaws. The begging:

                            In. In. In.

Michael Martin Shea

Rough Draft of a Poem About Heartbeats

Hers first. The beat of it. Something original, like a washing machine
or a car tire with two big nails in it. Describe the tire. It has to be black.

Describe changing the tire with your father and talk about his heartbeat,
which will involve the radio bump in his chest where the defibrillator is.

Pretend your father's heart is made of pennies. Mention that the wires
are copper—it won't make sense if you don't. Your father has high cholesterol

and your brother has high cholesterol and you are at risk for heart disease.
Your doctor says you have high triglycerides. Don't even bother trying to spell

that word. Spell check will fix it. Pretend that word is a wave you can dive
under. Pretend the whoosh of the wave is the sound hearts make. Realize

you've never heard your own heart with a stethoscope. Wonder if you can
get a stethoscope easily. Remember the time you snorted Adderall and sweat

through two t-shirts and a jacket as your heart pounded. Think of your heart
as a washing machine and the Adderall as Tide. Or Shout. Or OxiClean.

Think of your blood as a wardrobe. Imagine your heart trying on clothes in a mirror.
Wonder if a heart feels like an avocado. Remember that she likes to eat avocado

with lemon juice and nothing else. Think of how weird that is. Think of how
avocado leaves green slime on everything else in a salad. Wonder if blood

is like slime when it's inside you. Remember that blood is only red when oxygen
hits it. Realize that most of your blood will never see the light of day unless

you get stabbed. Think of your stabbing as your blood looking in the mirror
for the first time and realizing it has red eyes. Think of your heart as a vampire

that drinks itself. Wonder if everyone's blood tastes like pennies. Your father's,
especially. Hers too. Think of her neck as a part of the body that can never taste itself.

Allyson Paty

Score for the New Cotillion

do the knees	of the brother	in a stranger's	home video
when he chases	the dog	pulls	the dog's ears
do the left wrist	of an anchor	the right arm	of the riot cop
and the scalp	of the crowd	*c'mon*	do the pelvis
of the talent	in a blue movie	tilting always	away
add the torso	of a man	in the clip	from a prank
do the second	just before	he eats pavement	*you know*
you're a twisty	*little girl*	now switch	it's your neck
after the neck	of the brother	your shins	after the shins
of the anchor	your navel	of the police	and thighs
of the crowd	you've got	the elbows	of the talent
and your lips	*c'mon*	do the lips	of the person falling

Jennifer Moore

As a Debutante I Adjusted My Hatpin

In the year of Our Lord the Electric Chair,
in the year of the Boozehound and the Unhooked Corset,
a lick of salt troubled my tongue.
A lick troubled me into telling the green girls
how to swing from the hundred-footed maple,
and the drowning woman how to sink into the river's bed.
As with all things, the difficulty lies
in making maneuvers look effortless.

In this year of the Obvious Ankles, rouge is applied
with a heavy hand. Cheekbones are achieved
through sucking. Tired of tiny perfumes,
I want to be your *voix de ville*:
both weft and warp, motive and cue.
Watch as I unfurl a web from my wrist.
When it flies, the trapeze artist sets sail;
in each arm, a bunch of begonias. Look how she
tosses her stems to the ushers.

If the sideshow acts fall through—
the moon walkers, the cloud counters—give me a spoon.
I'll be the Depressor of Tongues, the one
to observe every soft palate. The candy-flossing crowd
opens wide, but the stagehand gives me the hook.

Now I play to the haircuts,
the last of the Disappointment Acts.
I'm the tooth that cuts the sucked cheek,
one of a thousand pennies sewn to the vaudevillian's gown.

nominated by the University of Illinois at Chicago Program for Writers

Erin Ganaway

Meds

They ask how I sleep and I say:
like summer preserves, wintering

behind a wall of paneled doors,
under quilted glass I lay dormant

as okra, blackberries and cornhusks,
dreams scattered like sunflower seeds

resisting packed clay before a farmer
takes to tilling, skunk striped and pursed

tight to memory. I wake to splintered
limbs, a still-born body laced in webs.

They say for now sanity is this
preservation cupboard, this flayed out

waiting for reason to surface
like the pressed lips of rain-soaked crops.

Bradley Harrison

Salvation History

In the cereal aisle there stands a man.
& inside that man is another man.
& inside the second man there sleeps
a pregnant ocelot. & inside the ocelot
a deflated kickball. & within the kickball a small
burnt tongue. & next to the burn a napalm
canister. & in the spilled jelly a monarch bathing.
& in the bath a cracked telescope. & inside the crack
an enormous hammer. & in the hammer a sense
of uncertainty. & in that sense a three-legged coyote.
& on its ghost limb walks Sylvia Plath. & in Sylvia Plath
a wine glass shattered. & within that shatter a demon
in love. & in that love an illegible constitution. &
in the blurred ink a modest
skyscraper. & in that skyscraper an elevator
shaft. & instead of an elevator voila the Pequod.
& deep in its hull is a brothel of clouds.
& deep in that brothel a masturbating virgin. & in her palm
a promise. & in the promise a cardboard box. &
in the box a flag stiff with blood. & in the blood
a murder of crows. & dressing the murder
is stretched lingerie.
& the fabric was worn by Jesus Christ.
& protected for centuries in a chimney

packed with snow. & in that snow is
a crocus of cocaine. & in the crocus
a coastline of television antennae. &
blowing on the beach is an untethered
answer. & within the answer slumbers a boy. He turns
over & over & over & over & over & over & over &
over & over & over

Christine Stroik Stocke

Circle

I can't tap my foot or I can with
No rhythm whatsoever as I write
I'm standing on shaky ground
Ever since you put me down the piano player sings.

You can't move the tables
I say to the man next to me as he scrapes one along the floor.
We can can. I know we can make it if we
Can can. We can can. He's singing now while
The woman in the circle—I write circle because that's what
He's singing—I mean wheelchair—she
Moves the moved circle—I mean table, and
Baby goes round in circles like a bird up in the sky.

Blues for the people and then New Orleans
Land of Collard Greens but I do not stand to help her.
I have no rhythm whatsoever.

Daniel Meltz

Intrinsic Marimbas

I had 45 minutes so I went
to my favorite shoelace store on East
59th where the shoelace boy's always
flirting with the hot cashier in her skin-
tight top, they're appealing, although they don't
exactly take me in, and then it's out
into the street again where nobody's
sure if it's drizzling enough to haul out
the umbrella, the crowds are staggering,
the tourists in the glass Apple ele-
vator, the arm-in-arm Brazilians, the
jaywalking bullies, the women in flip-
flops, toes serenely gripping, the man and
woman in gorgeous sweaters and matching
tans emerging from Bergdorf's, door held, two
big doormen with creased smiles and no sense of
pomp. I was here a couple months ago
at Doug's suggestion, it was drizzling then
too, he loves that little shoelace store, where
they also do shines and repairs, of course—
he was always saying "of course," which I
hated at first, it seemed so condescend-
ing, but then I came to understand his
odd expressions of delight. I do not

miss him but I miss the way he showed up
jumping and took off bouncing and looked at
me as if we were jackhammering side-
walk—worker and foreman, deep into sex.
But the crowds were exciting, the drama
of the crisscross, and then a walk through Crate
and Barrel, I bought a pillow, black and
green, two men helped me, one large one small, both
Filipino, a double-barreled cruise
that only added to the jolt of the
purchase, they put my pillow in a see-
through bag which made me a little embar-
rassed. I thought, Let me take 58th back
west to get away from the people but
after a block I was bored, I wanted
to see the trees, so I circled around
and into the park where everything was
shockingly green from all the rain of this
week and the barks were black—greens and blacks as
exciting as the black and green of the
pillow I'd bought—the lindens in flower,
smelling like Juicy Fruit, soil, sopping,
mossy, quiet, the dark pain of quiet
so close to all the traffic, an awesome
Chartres with spandrel branches and stained-glass
leaves and fog in the spandrels, the fog's been
settled in among the building tops for
days, so unusual in midtown, you
can't see the top of Time-Warner, it
disappears into the fog along with

the top of the ugliest Trump in the
world and the memory of a boat ride
in the snow. Later, there he was, Doug, in
front of CVS, whispering my
name before he slipped inside.

nominated by upstreet

Jenny Gropp Hess

Months After the Crash, the Blind Aerobatic Pilot Speaks

Black box, my secret kin
before the nose-dive jammed

my body into the hat. I was no eel
when I hit the ocean's surface—now I am land

with the Braille, cattle under my fingers
this summer, my body on the mattress,

sweat drying into pounds,
as blank a house inside as out.

I am suitcases in a tremendous sea,
the exterior part of a vehicle

in this absurd custom of missing myself
like a radio program once recorded live.

I met a young man who lost his leg in battle
and he said distinct from his substance

his name saved him, worn thing.
Blood can't be stored for more than 42 days

but my vision still reds out in rapid climbs,
inverted spins, Cuban eights, in remembrance

I get outside a bottle of whiskey, back
on the outside of the curve, amphitheater

turned inside out, no possibility
of grabbing the door handle

and feeling someone turn it from the other side,
no possibility of translating flight dry and husky

when the side of the wing is in line
with the rest of the world, upper limit,

my face whitening, a breaker in air—
in 1932 the Royal Air Force trained men

to fly with a hood over the cockpit, take off,
turn over, spin and dive, straighten out blind,

a wave covered in mud, mud covered
in waves, shells covered in mud must slide

in paths visible for tenths of a second, blindness
begetting blindness, a jet passing open-jawed making paste

of birds at the speed of men
gathering acres in the radar nest, turning

like a sparrow entering through a window, mistaking
the space between floor and ceiling for sky.

nominated by the University of Alabama

Janet McNally

Maggie Leaves the Underworld

We saw her for weeks in our dreams, a slim ghost
crossing the street in ski boots. Her strides

were plastic, doll-kneed, and the snow
fell like postcards, bleeding purple

in the neon. Quiet. There are dead girls
who come back, their hearts bruised as plums

on the orchard floor, late September. Some secret
flint sparks their beating and they stretch, they rise.

By spring, she'd thrown all her miracles
like white doves in magic tricks. Her last dreams

were wildflowers, periwinkle and ochre, dipped
in the sort of useless pollen that gathers

on windowsills instead of bee's legs. She came
back, she breathed in, her slate eyes opened.

It was some kind of show. We presented
her to strangers, but she never told

the truth while we were listening. We asked her
to open her mouth

wide enough for us to see the birds inside,
the seeds strung like garnets

on silken thread. Imagine, we said,
her throat as it opens. Imagine everything

she had to swallow before she convinced them
to let her go.

Victoria Lynne McCoy

Self-Portrait in Unfinished Letters

Dear—
      The gulf is bleeding   black
                                  again.
They say they'll fix it. They say Claude Chabrol is dead
               for the first time
        today—September 12th and church bells
                  through the courtyard window.
           I meant to see more of his films
while he was alive. Barreling down Pacific Coast Highway,
      what was that song? Do you remember
           what Allison sounds like sitting shotgun?

                +

Dear—
      I quit vegetarianism last month.
Remember when the teacher said,
          I'm too old to protest?
        The largest picture on the front page
            of the paper is a man crossing Bryant Park
with a mannequin
                underarm. They said
       they'd fix it. A city of moths
         to the tent-white sheen of celebrity.

I try to leave her
out of this one: Allison, a choir of whispers in the dark.

+

Dear—
They decided not to burn the Quran yesterday.
You've always liked it better when there's a *they* in the story.
I've lost faith in my own

impact.

The Nile is drowning in one hundred tons
of gasoline and Allison is dead
for the one thousand seven hundred seventeenth time
when I wake. There's a fire

under the earth they can't fix.

+

Dear—
La fille cupée en deux in a near-empty theater.
my appendages haunted

with so many almosts.

I've forgotten her face for the third time today.

A sunken-in man on the subway sings about a city
built entirely of instruments that make

no sound.

The train doors open
their ghost-bright mouths, a calling—

I'll go anywhere
the sirens can't find me.

Chuck Carlise

A Compendium of Photographs: L'Inconnue de la Seine

1. Stock photograph of unidentified death mask, Paris
Date & source unknown

> *mask faces viewer, direct. light from stage-left creates movement in shadows*
> *at eyes & chin, illusion of slight head-cock, blush in cheeks. plaster build-up*
> *in hairline & lashes below right eye. no notes, identifying marks on print.*

These are the first days, when recollection is meaningless—
        when everything is a new lesson; before
    the sidelong glance, before suspicion.
There is so much you still want to believe. Does it
        damage you more to learn
     you are mortal, or not to?
   The most primal act
      begins in the face: to face something. Responsibility.
        She turns; she is turned.
The self doesn't have a face—the body does.

2. "L'Inconnue de la Seine" from Undying Faces: A Collection of Death Masks
Ernst Benkard; 1927

> *face upright, slight turn right so left cheek is in fore; hair is thin,*
> *wispy. light source above, dim; forehead & nose framed in its glare.*
> *she seems smaller here. behind, backdrop is a clean, unbroken black.*

Now she is named: Unknown of the Seine. It happens here.
L'Inconnue, a stranger. From *connu*—as *cognition*. & its lack.
Dispossessed, even in name; remembered as forgotten.
It's Benkard who coins it—imagining her *feeble shoulders, burned wings.*
Last face in his roll—after Newton, Napoleon, Wagner, Lenin.
L'Inconnue; say it like *ingénue* (stock character—
innocent, wholesome, doe-eyed girl).
Butterfly at a flame, he calls her. Then simply, *unknown*.

3. "La Vierge inconnue, du canal de l'Ourcq"
Albert Rudomine; 1927

> *lens closer, slightly raised; light is striking—neck in shadow. visible bulb of eye or
> saw-dust beneath eyelids. high cheekbones emphasized, demure smile. proximity
> to subject creates an intimacy; gray shading on lower lip almost suggests color.*

Anonymous Virgin is a game of language—sex, yes; also
                              Holy Mother Unknown.
             Rudomine knew. Knew light on the body, anyway.
      His others, his nudes, always in extremis—lightplay on muscle—
often without faces (heads turned away,
                    shadow obscuring)—the body as itself,
      as movement in space, struggle contained. Never
a narrative—just object, surface, reflection
                          of light. By now she is famous—
      bodiless starlet, a romance. This is the shot they'll remember her for.

4. "Roger & Marcel Lorenzi, Workshop at Rue Racine"
Lorenzi Moulder Archive; 1960

> *two men at worktable; clay splotches, shelves of masks (a blur). five faces on table, various states of completion (one not yet cut from clay block). closest to lens, l'Inconnue, directly below light source, powerful glare; most of her features not visible.*

To be hidden in plain sight. To be exposed. We know
      she's a mask. This is no secret.
This is *where*. This is *how*. This room, these hands.
          There is nothing behind the fantasy
& so nothing lost. It only hides the void,
            the nothing, the lack in the viewer.

5. Untitled portrait of Ewa Lazlo, rumored to have been l'Inconnue
Photographer unknown; c.1890s?

> *pale-skinned woman in elaborate formal dress (feather hat, corsages, parasol);*
> *painted backdrop (forest scene?). resemblance to mask is evident. open eyes*
> *make comparison difficult. they seem preoccupied—she knows something.*

Fame is also a story we tell ourselves: to be loved
is to be loved. Hungarian showgirl, some said was the face—
    played Paris, then murdered touring Chile.
Another self that won't answer, won't correct. In London, this year,
they're staging it; Ewa Lazlo the star, the unknown. Every bit of it, turns out,
    false. Admitted. *Made it all up.* Possibility
        is another romance. So familiar
    as to be nearly unrecognized.

6. Cover sequence (for the novel, Aurélien, by Louis Aragon)
Man Ray; 1944

camera over her shoulder; soft light. facing a mirror, an inch (no more) from own reflection. double image somehow creates sense of agency, intention. she appears to be humming or trying to remember something.

Mirrors are a way to trick a body
          that has lost a part of itself—a phantom limb that aches,
     that twitches, that burns. A confusion of the mind:
  you see vacancy, a space you no longer occupy.
               You understand this, but memory persists, insists
it knows where the body ends. It is wrong. So: the mirror.
          The mind sees two; the pain recedes.
  Not all illusions are lies; not all lies are empty.

7. Cover sequence (for the novel *Aurélien*, by Louis Aragon)
Man Ray; 1944

> *eyes. black lace veil draped over forehead, neck, suggests clothing, body, shoulders. eyes*
> *open, superimposed in narrow band, searching past viewer (concerned, skeptical).*
> *below them, smile is somehow different. beginnings of grimace, lip-bite, reanimate.*

Creation, in most cases, is more rearrangement. At core
                we're still the same cocktail of metals & gases—the human body,
                            the coffee mug, the stars. It's boxer's wisdom
        that you can't hold someone's eye without punching or kissing—
                    the two edges of defense; how we learn
            who's in charge. It's not from seeing or being seen, but the electricity—
                the eyes & the eyes & what's created between them.

8. "L'Inconnue de la Seine, 94euro" inventory image
Lorenzi Moulders; 2012

>*white mask facing forward, hooked to clapboard drywall. bright, indoor light.*
>*a product for sale. in low-wattage lighting, chin appears fuller; face appears*
>*younger. caption declares: mask can be lacquered or (like this one) matte.*

One way to understand the cold: absence of heat.
                    Not a condition; a default. Everything is cold
        until heat intrudes. Which is also to say, nothing.
    There are states of rest, irreducible, that would endure
                without contingency (that is, without addition
                        of heat, of color, of narrative arc).
To purchase an object is to invite alteration, to pursue it.
        On a wall or laid flat on a table,
    she is just plaster, textured to ridges & shape. White is color
                & the absence of color; snow or the hottest stars.

Michele Poulos

Thursdays in the Faubourg Marigny

Would slink out of the house at midnight
done for Vaughan's Lounge,
that piece of down-home-dirty,
swagger through New Orleans avenues
thick with Mississippi steam,
black slip dress slit up the side, black
tights battered with snags, powdered,
baked, glittered, the night
holding its soft wrists open.
Easy as the club's silver notes that slid
across the sidewalk and through barbeque
smoke, meat cooked out of the back
of a pick-up truck, tin foil glinting
like the teeth of that man in the alley.
I fed him his hot sauce, thumbprint of red
whorled on each nipple, hips peaked
like bald cypress knees, his mouth
pulling at my breast as though refusing
isolation, as if I could lay bare
each burrowed place inside him, the sucking
at first hard, then pleading and reckless
as the staggered walk back to his place
where for hours we fucked in full dark
penetrated by the cheap blue neon

wailing across the street, a sign whose light
scattered across the skeleton mask
he'd slipped on: bulbous forehead,
grid of teeth, eyes hollow as a gouge
of earth, nose an upside-down heart.
It was death come knocking,
night-winged and thieving, and all I gave
was stars kindled, body flown.

Harry Bauld

Black Icarus

Fallen Angel, Basquiat, 1981

When he lights, when he touches down
> *out of no pastel effing blue*

the clouds will speak in their grey tongues
> *out of roar and glide you cannot imagine*

the prophecy of the fathers who gave him blood wax and white wings
> *out of your own mess of ground*

but now the bird of this brush with revelation rises
> *from the blue filth which is my only frame*

and he sees through our two transparent dimensions
> *come to tear the tenemented clawmarks*

with black lenses that burn the blue pretentions
> *into your walls and facades against my return*

to ash, with the baby eyes of his undescended balls
> *come to pitch and fork you*

his stall-scratched genitals drawn up the center, a gyroscope
> *to go where they say you can't go*

into the transparent trunk of missing organs
> *in the dash and dot of my own message*

under the fir that carves its unbroken code into the sky
> *on wings to take us off with, you and me*

and his desperate white talon will land
> *into the only destination worth a damn*

if we have patience when something feathers us over and over
> *to you, O wingless and longing, O my brother.*

Timothy Daniel Welch

On the Isle of Erytheia

My virginity, like a herd of red cattle
                I drove for seventeen years,

was dumb and almost

        beautiful—
           I spent my time tending

to the animals in me. I remember their tails,
              those tender curls, and

        the long nights
following strays to the rim

          of town and faltering, spooked

               by a train whistle or the start
      of an engine. Some place, this

Erytheia, for skinny boys
         without a sense of butchery—

      a tiny island of Greek heroes
who came to kill whatever

sad, hoofing creatures insulted

the gods. Then the myth

of my own hard slaughter: there was
            a girl, she led me to a vacant life

guard tower, told me to begin with the shirt
                  or the pants, my inadequacy was

      a Homeric round-up.

Against the silver-rooted water
      the sky reddened

           and blackened itself, a little
breeze crept calmly along

      the sand and dropped grain
               after grain into its golden bowl.

Cate Lycurgus

Taking Care

We thought   that we   could solve

all things   that pine sol-/vent   could

so prevent not on   ly dirt   but

break-ing down   through mak-

ing good   the liv-er breaks to

make a liv   ing be/

ing breaks   enzymes

in time   it too dis-/solves de-

volves denatures and   it is the na-

ture of what is a/live   and even

bile   the yellow   O the

yell-ow   bile is beaut-/y

full in O of all the living it allows

and so   and so   don't pine

don't pin pine on   what will

not   sol/ve not   an-

ything not when   a liv/er will

not be a/live-   r an-   ymore

Corey Van Landingham

Tabernacle for an Adolescence

The science experiments gone awry. The skulls of vermin
and the black silk ribbon strung through them. The lamp
she tied them to. The light she never left on. The place
to bury cicada husks. The place to buy purple face glitter.
The surface disorder. The forest and that one clearing
swollen and yellow through the hacksaw trees. The sexy
forest where she chose one man over another with her
mouth. The fizz in the medicine. The stomach of noise.
The faucets rusted out on the side of the house like sentinels.
The flood lights turned off. The lake with all those leeches.
The way they mirrored fucking—find something and attach
yourself. The dock built in the middle of the lake she could never
bring herself to swim to. The fish that appeared to be drowning.
The uncanny light on the teeth they never had. The water plants
recoiled so as not to have to touch her skin. The scream
in the middle of the night in the town she forgot owned her.
The hoot of the train as it mocked her staying there. The apples
she whittled into pipes and the weed she forgot in another state.
The lunch she forgot at her desk and the mold on the wheat
bread. The man on the trolley who told her he'd certainly
save her if she was drowning. The microscope her mother
practiced scrutiny on. The antidote to all those pills she was
taking. The walls with scrawled song lyrics and the irony in the
rap music she memorized. The foreign exchange student and

all her cigarettes. The stuffed owl in her grandmother's house.
The little boxes she collected. The boxes made in woodshop to
hide her pills. The forest her father drove into to take her home.
The dress he made her out of an old tweed jacket to hide her
bare body. The instruments her mother used to pick her apart.
The camera her father set up in the living room to reconstruct
her face. The birthday cake slapped on her lap and the sleeves
of the dress dragging in the chocolate frosting. The candles fallen
to the carpet around her socks and the fire she might have been
able to stomp out, had she not been still in the forest, a stump
of a girl. The fire that started every time she came home and all
those photographs nuzzled into her hand when she woke up
in the trees. The mouths of fish hung above her. Proof
she was not some experiment. The proof that she was.

Matthew Nienow

O Anchor

Dark charms the anchor in its house

of water and what type of bottom
it drags, for what type of work, for you,

with your need to stay in roughly the same place

for a night, with your questions of how
much to let out

and how well your windlass works

and how you feel sometimes hauling
200 foot of chain by hand in the dark,

wondering what in your life sent you

here, where the world exists as much
below you as above; where you are

as much the chain as the chain.

Oliver Bendorf

I Promised Her My Hands Wouldn't Get Any Larger

But she's decided we need to trace them in case I
turn out to be wrong. Every morning she wakes me
with a sheet of paper. In the beginning, she stowed
all the tracings in a folder, until one day I said *I'd like
to at least see where this is going*, and from that point on
we hung them on the wall chronologically. When I
study them, they look back at me like busted
headlights. I wear my lab coat around the house to
make sure they know who's observing whom. If we
can ensure records, if we can be diligent in our
testing. I wrap my fingers around her wrist. Nothing
feels smaller yet. Not her, not the kettle nor the key.
If my hands do grow, they should also be the kind
that can start a fire with just a deer in the road.

Tory Adkisson

Homosexuality

Desire, I drape over my chest
so you know what flag I bear,
what nation I want to land on
when the rescue workers
& newscasters have pulled me
from the dark, allowing me to
rinse my foliate feathers, shed
my oily skin—& with wings
steeped in fire, they won't be able
to look at me—the light would burn
pinholes in their pupils—
& what they will ask as they kneel
is *How long does the bridge run*
in your heart, how deliberately
dark is the birdcage. I will give them
an answer & after they've kissed
my feet, I will give them a pair
of sunglasses, so when I sit down
to eat they'll be able to see clear
through my throat to the window
behind it & wait their turn to
bring a knife & fork to the table.

Aviva Englander Cristy

The Measure of Vessel and Nerve

1. Vessels

> The air in London therefore is always heavy, and in autumn particularly so.
> —William Harvey, *The Anatomy of Thomas Parr,* 1635

My body is a hollow craft, basin
and burrow. This passage a fluent
inventory to limbs, repetition
of form and circumnavigation that
achieves fourfold the earth's perimeter.
My median cubital vein remains
unfathomable, sending the insistent
syringe on, foraging for another
vessel. A violation of dermis
brings blood surfacing, the needle incise
each blue deposit to loose constraint
and cadence against elasticity.
My body is a fading bruise, each vein
a measure, the eloquence of winter.

2. *Lungs*

> The *substance* of the lung is of a light, porous, spongy texture; it floats in water and crepitates when handled, owing to the presence of air in the tissue.
> —*Gray's Anatomy*

Wings flutter, pocked with alveoli
intuiting a butterfly determined.
I learned late in life that I was breathing
backwards; with each intake my diaphragm
constricting, a shrinking box against light
and sky. I must concentrate intention
on the chamber and thread of breath, feel
the undertow of air against exposed lips.
An inhale should widen cavities. Pressure
vacuum accompanies metered thrum as
each bronchioles offers unobstructed
navigation from element to blood.
An exhale compresses membranes,
purges desolation, as the lungs redden.

3. *The Seventh Nerve*

> So talented are we at reading people's faces that the imperceptible becomes
> perceived.
>>—Charles Hodgson, *Carnal Knowledge*

The nerve to open; the vulnerable
face. When the seventh nerve fails
the face falls lax, a motionless manifest.
There is an excess of fibers here
extended towards response and memory,
nerves paired against a slackening bias.
An excess of bodies contained, fashion
and partition of each fragmented sense.
Our souls prevail, sequenced, unique
as habit, the conventional shiver
carried, not in time but courage,
not a conduit but proof. The human
anima verified, housed in dermis.
We witness the absent body unsecured.

4. *Incision*

> In the bloodless animals, however, the heart beats very slowly and at long intervals
> and in the manner of other animals' hearts that are a-dying.
> —William Harvey, *Movement of the Heart and Blood in Animals*, 1628

In a single moment blades press flat to skin.
Once, just before, I felt this edged desire.
You see, the hand must always remember
the human. This is why we practice
here, with flesh pink and firm, the blood thick,
the softness just inside the thigh.
Feel resistance, the need to press harder.
Train your hands to pressure open a surface
without tearing, without the rush of doubt.
Imagine a rose. Each petal wilts
when pulled apart, the next one softly
losing perfection when exposed to light.
Yes you will pause before you break man's flesh,
your hand will still in wonder at a friend.

Shevaun Brannigan

Why My Mother is Afraid of Heights

When the servant held her by her ankles
          upside down off the roof   like she was

a bird he was plucking,   feathers
        flying in clumps through the streets of India,   like the dandelion fluff

from home   that you blew to make a wish like
        I wish he doesn't drop me   *I wish this hadn't*

happened,   this being   the molesting, the threats, then   -to come-
the disbelief,   when a girl came forward and said   *he made me*

touch him,   and she, my mother, said *me too,* they told her she was
a naughty girl who just wanted attention,   like that was always

      such a crime, to want your parents   to look at what they had made,
what the body was doing, what   was being done to the body,   it was

too much to ask, and she   always was asking   for someone to
   love her, just   a little bit, and   they believed the first girl, who

must not have been held   over the roof, if she was telling,   she was older, heavier,
perhaps he couldn't   hoist her up and display her   like the flag,

but when he held my mother   by her ankles   while below her, the open dumpster's
            mouth yawned,   spun around,

waited to receive her body,   to swallow her up,   this made the case, she knew
        the bags of trash would not   cushion her fall, she was learning

at that very moment   the mass of her body   was immense, all sixty three pounds
        would plummet,   she was learning   to have a body

was a gift, to have a body   was to have a weapon,   was to
        be desired and that you could control   nothing, not even

which way was up.

Jeff Oaks

Saint Wrench

1

The more you see a thing the less you see it, the more it quiets into a minor character, an unnamed member of the Greek chorus as it turns and counter-turns, while you soliloquize in the bathroom over the broken toilet seat about your own helplessness. Your own face alights on itself as the bowl refills, sighs, stops quivering. Here is the moment a hero is made, you think.

2

It is possible to imagine that the name Christ written in the sand by the first nervous devotees was not a fish but a wrench, a single form drop-forged, capable of removing bent nails from good wood, of turning suddenly the water back on after days of drought and renovation.

3

In the wrench's slippery eye the universe revolves around the earth. It doesn't recognize Galileo's cosmology as weight-bearing. A wrench dreams of holding and being held, of being the instrument by which things are made to turn, until everything is adjusted. It doesn't sing. It makes a minor silver clink. Opened, it's Hathor, the old moon goddess, her glittering horns.

4

Each face is made up of a pair of minor faces, one that angles up, one that looks down its nose. Forced together they grow hungry for something to talk about. They will latch onto anything. Your fingernails, for instance. Your teeth. Anything to make you start.

nominated by Poemeleon

Ross White

Ocean Quahog

Researchers in Wales say they have discovered the world's oldest living creature – a 405-year-old clam.
—ABC News

Done counting rings, scientists claim the clam
has lived four centuries. Poor sod, all that time,
he never planned a trip, just mouth open
to where the currents took him.
That's a long time to lug a home around,
but home is where the heart, kidney, and anus are,
wherever the open circulatory system pumps.
He deserves credit for persistence, but acknowledge
the difficulty of a clam giving up. How would it look
any different? Left in his bed, in the arctic deep,
long enough, undisturbed by shark or squid,
living must be the surrender.

Paul Hlava

For Anna on the Day a Man Flashed Her on the Beach

You walked where the gates were closed and locked
corrugated steel spray-painted
with names you said you couldn't read   and didn't want to
pit bulls followed you   from inside the fence
their genetic desire for order   through harm
was an audible boiling inside their massive chests
the kids rides collected silence
it rained and then it stopped   even now you carry that fluid
you are the shape of your mother
and wear her crescent hips like a runaway carriage
pulling the sun over the Atlantic   you moved
through the loose newspaper alleys   to the sand
where you curled your feline body in your hooded coat   and fell asleep
a day later I found sand in your pockets   your tiny canvas shoes
I laughed at the sand in your hair   your long hair that also
was everywhere   strands clung to the shower tile
were draped across my wire coat hangers
once I woke in the morning and pulled one from my beard
for just a moment I thought it was mine
thread by thread you were losing yourself
to become the mosquitoes that hovered above us as we slept
who nursed their eggs on our blood
in the diminishing gardens of our consciousness blue babies
grappled jellyfish   you looked out at the lunar rhythm of the waves

sand covered your wrists   the webs between your fingers
when you heard the pst
the voice said, pst   and when you turned
he was laying on his side masturbating into the sand
I ordered the appetizer plate   you ordered a flight of wine
the sun rose and set like a glass falling infinitely on the inside
you'd just forgot to mention it you said
was I a background character in the movie of your life
we were two abused servants
of knowing and not-knowing   bosses who demanded overtime
who told us what we walk around thinking   is hardly important
everyone is pulled eventually to sleep
by the weight of birdshot in their hearts
while the sky races inside its frame
water rushing over rocks   the boulders you carry home
in the pockets of your coat
while the sky races inside its frame
first it's humid   then it hails
someone's car skids on an ice-patch on the outskirts of the city
we exist inside a purple attic   the streets are anything
but reliable   where the man yanked the woman by the arm
I couldn't understand
the language of their screaming   he shook her
and jerked her into the road   were there more men like him
inside the opened doorway
her ankle scraped the asphalt inside his guttural cursing
I continued my approach on the sidewalk
if he raises his fist
if he raises his open hand
whose business is anyone's personal affairs anyway

people can be trees   or motes pulled from a sunburned shoulder
if he pushes her   if he shakes her one more time
am I enough of a man
he spit in her face and left   and she left
and I walked to the liquor store   as it had been planned
we are hardly a great generation
our moral certainties that penciled flight plans over the Atlantic to
Normandy
have been deciding what is worth forgetting
of course you walked away from him Anna
and continued along the broken shore   where the ocean became
a multi-eyed creature   who swallows children whole
but don't worry about it   it happens, you said
all uncertain possible happenings were drifting to the eddies of your hair
around your ears and neck were sheaves of timber   plastic bags
oil-slicked paddling sea otters   foaming at their broken teeth
a waiter dropped a tray of ginger ales
and a patron slipped   toward the marble corner of the bar
and reached out and caught himself
the little dangers we grow accustomed to
collect and deepen   in the bathroom mirror   we wash our faces in it
and brush our teeth   and hold it unawares between our gums and lips
as we walk out into the morning
you said it happened to you also as a girl
just last month a car stopped at an intersection   the door swung open
where a man revealed himself to Chloe   what is our purpose here
in the cellar of tolerance a man is plucking out my beard
until he reaches the muscles of my jaw
and pushes through
to find wires that make me move

I want to make you a rustle of leaves   caught in the lungs of a robin
but my wanting anything is a variance of danger
we could disappear
a ghost town near an old closed silver mine
the facade of the adobe jail chipping   the no visitors sign
carried off by a sand storm
you could be that negative space in the dust
subject to the same blackouts   bill collectors   swarms of locusts
helmeted Mormons would still cross the tracks
stop for a handful of water at the pump   shoot the cans
we set up at the rim of the well
rain would come   soil migrate beneath us
invisibly rearranging the cuneiform bones of dinosaurs
tract homes sprouting in beautiful Euclidean geometry
the fat baby of providence pulled wet and crying from a sewer drain
the crowd goes wild   the fireman wipes mud from its brow
and hands it to its mother   Anna
it's been said a woman's greatest honor is to suffer   do you agree
that within one sea there is another   placid beneath the sun's reach
sulfide waves beneath the waves   lap a hydrothermal vent
blind fish weave through tube-worms at its base
the system was the system of ages
it moved in crystal threads about our heads
beyond our sense of dream or touch   we were born from that place of pain
and I find your hair inside my computer case   woven into the rug
pressed inside Autobiography of Red   did I eat a strand in my scrambled eggs
they scurry along the baseboard   to the labyrinth behind the walls
they are everywhere because they are nowhere   I see them
out the window perched on the bare branches
of course you stood up and moved away   the image

is a calcified beak   that spears a minnow
through itself   reflected on that wavering world
it lifts into the air   and the shadow is for a moment giant
you walk inside of it   where a wind picks up the surface of the beach
a change too small for anyone to notice
a yellowish cloud that rises and falls   and remains
a grit in your collar   a disturbance in the creases of your shoes

Meghan Privitello

Again, Let's Do It Again

Let's start over. I will be a pilgrim wife and you will drive the wagon. We'll give the oxen doomsday names like Steel and Ore. When the food runs out we will feast on each other's bodies like there was a hole in our brains where *cannibalism* should be, like we were trying to erase the old king's idea of love. I will brew tea over the fire until I singe my cheeks you will call me a dirty wife without expecting anything extra when your pants are down. We will cry at brown rivers. We will fear any height greater than us. Let me start over. You are a husband. I am a wife. We are in love we are not in love. We eat sleep like it's something familiar. We starve ourselves for days. When we wake up we forget each other's names and spend the rest of the day flipping through the alphabet like it could make us assemble. We are too new-world to understand that our armoire's tongue and groove is what gets museums hard. You, what gets you hard? I am hardly a beast when it comes to bedrooms when it comes to you, bridegroom. I find it hard to believe that we were not made in a factory. The way we touch each other without improvisation. The way I always look at you, adoringly, on time. If we start over as two strangers whose history is written in lemon juice, how many nights are you willing to sacrifice trying to decipher my dainty code? How can we love each other with so much skin in the way? In an orange grove, we could be two oranges that touch. Finally, we could depend on the farmer to gather us in the same crate, on the child to be hungry enough to unpeel us and eat us both at once.

Sarah Green

What to Expect When You Become a Motel Balcony

Whoever you were, now you're just wood
shoulder-to-shoulder with other wood, day
laborers in line. A balcony is just

a floor raised off the ground. The sun warms
mossy wood more slowly than bleached wood;
try to slant in rain.

No one inspects your joists. A balcony is
just a floor with a railing. Meanwhile, gutters
spew exuberantly. Doves and robins

busy the air with chirping. Remember
dotted swiss. Remember morning's white blouse…

Even cast-off straw a dove flies carrying in its
mouth can bend to make a nest. Your
wood slats splay, a Spanish fan, a hand of

playing cards. Between your rails, the air's
empty as a drinking glass.

nominated by Ohio University

Meggie Monahan

No Such Thing as Acceptance

You can button your grief in a new wool coat and walk it down to the sea.
You can anchor your feet in the sand to watch it drown itself in cold daylight
and after it's over, wrap your arms around yourself and try to remember its body.

Where does it hurt? he asked. She placed his palm on her chest. He felt no pulse.
Parted lips, tilted chin. *Show me where it hurts* he repeated. She unbuttoned her pants.
On the news, a drive-by shooting. Reporters said it could have been anybody.

School girls take turns spitting their cherry pits into sewer grates. Subway tunnels
trace a dim constellation of fate. 41 days since my husband left. *I will walk around naked
more often. I will not wear my hair in a bun.* All of my offers whispered to nobody.

Open the bedroom window. Stare down at the flicked sidewalk cigarette butts
from hundreds of sticky nights tangled in white linens, the kind reserved
for the dead. Remember the dark smell of yourself coming alive, the way a body

refuses to break when loved into an openness it cannot hold. There is no such thing
as acceptance. There is only standing on a shoreline, writing a name in water.
There is only squinting in the morning light, praying you recognize somebody.

Michael Roche

Story with a Heart-Shaped Hole in It

The Bible talks about frogs falling from the sky. The Book of Michael, if there ever is one, will tell the story of *The Heart-Shaped Hole in My Umbrella*. It will go like this: Not even I could believe it was a beating heart that fell from the sky and tore a hole in my umbrella during the rainstorm. Nevertheless, I picked it up and started walking to the nearest hospital to see if it might be used in a transplant. Right then, another heart hit me on the head before landing on the sidewalk. Angrily, I threw my torn umbrella to the side of the road and carefully picked up the heart, cupping it gently in my hands and brushing a piece of gravel off the left ventricle. In a junkyard to my left was a rusty unicycle I started riding. Once I balanced myself, I began juggling the two hearts with my left hand. The mailman cheered me on. Some pedestrians complimented my form. When I arrived at the hospital, I handed the hearts over to a team of cardiologists who poked them in various places. The doctors proved they were indeed hearts and not some kind of soft-tissue meteorite. The police, of course, had questions for me. I rode with some officers to the scene of my abandoned umbrella. Six more hearts had fallen in the vicinity. Some neighborhood boys were pelting them at each other.

Gale Marie Thompson

Bodega

I am concerned about the bodega. I want to get it down, to be limited by these cold stars, to walk with cigarettes by the bodega. Our families are there, fundamentally unchanged and received with gladness by the bodega. It's nights like this when I get cranky and wish for bad weather. I can't stand it when you tell me bodega. I'm such a baby in the dark blue periphery. I cried on the bus as we passed the bodega, my feet still above the hallway, not at all feeding the best parts of me. There is a plastic bag of cilantro wilting in the bodega and right now, at this very second, everyone else is growing a little bit taller. Everything's settling before I can get to it. Here I am by the bodega recording beyond what I can record at any given time. I see towns like they are not, films like they are not. Here now I am remembering you by the bodega. Here now I bought you a book although you are not here.

Martin Rock

Double Acrostic for Francis Ponge

For at the heart of the uniform, reasoning is shaky and elusive:
a mind in search of ideas should first stock up on appearances.

Faceless boar split on the spit: abracadabra
or objective correlative made manifest:
reverently, I peel off the animal's dermis: I am
          beholden to its pigment: Spiritus Mundi
absolves the crime: what woman
throws herself at the knife: what man is dead

to sit in the house of featureless scholars: there is no I
here: nor can he claim himself extinct: that a fin
extinguished on some great fish's trunk:

                                         that an ass
hee-hawed to believe itself a horse: it is in objects we
ease into ourselves: the slit bark   holds inside a flea
attenuating itself to a simple thought: with her
rear-legs she withdraws from the scene: elliptic
tailor: flat as a fallen leaf: she marks the skin to stitch

or suck the sutras out: her body of water is empty too:
feckless hole where the earth has taken itself away: staff

to be pointed towards the slippery bank: over the fire I
heave the pig around the branch: the trees are naked

edits of themselves: surgery that happens only once
            & is done: I mutter *cageot* & a fuchsia
utterance falls as a leaf & dissolves: into moist moss
not even an echo can survive:
I am to eat the pig: I am to eat humanity's
formlessness: I am to eat you, M. Ponge: your ash
on the tongue is moist as a pod: your tongue an embryo
reasserting itself from beneath a crust of words: you
make things happen: or things have made you   to spill
                                  their names to the ground
ripe as rotten fruit untouched by man:
ear-shaped & hollow as the ear: the fallen leaf
alone rots beneath his rotting twins: c a s t r a t i
stolen from the bath: a hoax: kingly feast of boar
opened to reveal hot moisture: bland: the earth's axis
now skewers the flesh of the hog: lift   the   skirt
I have woven: reveal the slippery hollow:
notch the machiner's belt: & now to stave: nouns
gestate inside their objects & become verbs: are meat
                                  signifiers so
insignificant as to lack nutrition: let suck the Doric
stock: marrow from the femur's column: cock
sounding himself into existence on the farm: *coteau-coteau*
has split the hillock: pressed language's button: keep
an eye to the sea:
keep the hollow ear beneath the slippery tongue: O
you, M. Ponge, most of all have made me see: the bun

alone regrets its shape: the masculine rock contains anima
nestled in its hard & frigid womb: the orange's pulp

despises itself for having been plump pods of juice:　　steep
　　　　deeply, o tea, to hide the water's transparent ache:
excitedly I'll drink:　　and feel her moisture on my chin:　　a
leavened bread reveals its form as cultures burn:　　the star
unearthed from its housing:　　beak from bird:　　ephemera
sleeps with no man:　　what ends must first slip:　　I plan
inwardly to eat the boar:　　thick and grizzled hair:　　barbaric
veins that pump word-blood to the floor:　　what knows me
ends:　　what knows me not, knows this:　　the form extends

Ben Purkert

Ode to Stretch Armstrong

Didn't you ever fling him across the mud room?
All these rules around a body, how far it can
or cannot. Stretch could land hard & never look,
so to speak, thrown. Like a pronoun, he'd leap
rivers to attach to something else.
Don't you lose him! (in the heat vents by the door)
Somewhere you can bet more of Stretch's
being made. Every moment on the assembly line
is itself assemblage: hands gluing on the legs,
or virtually no hands at all, only the sun,
which is also a machine. Once a Boy
Scout on your block had nine gold screws
inserted in his shin. Once, on TV, a copter flew
so low to the earth, it missed it entirely.

Rebecca Bauman

The Dwarf Hamster

June - October, 1990

Tell Ms. Ward you did not suffer.
Say that when I carried you
from the playroom to the bathroom,
that when I squeezed you like a water balloon
and threw you to the floor—
say you bit me first.

Some night, when she is brushing her teeth
and all the little juice-boxes seem miles away,
you should appear atop her soap dish,
a baby carrot half-stuffed into your cheek.
Let your eyes glint like caviar. Let her see
that your world is now a good place

beyond the small, overzealous hands
blotted with dried paste. Let her see you
unmolested, standing upright on small white feet—
a brazen tuft of afterlife. Give her peace
as surely as you still give me grief, as readily
as she banished me, horrified,
from the rabbit and box turtle, too.

She must know
I did not understand;
when I returned the soft round of your remains
to those pine shavings long-steeped in urine,
I had no reason to believe anyone would notice
you'd ever left the room.

Kasandra Larsen

What to Say When You Come Home to Find Him Wearing Your Clothes

Wow. That bra never really fit me right,
but you look great. That shade lights up your eyes.
I saved those garters for a special night;
why not now? We needed a fresh surprise,
admit it. We got routine, so boring.
Grab that dress off the bed. Give it a twirl.
See how it drapes? You know, I've been thinking—
biology begins us all as girls
in the womb. A man who remembers that?
Sexy. Your thoughts make you desirable,
not just your body. No, you don't look fat.
I'm sorry. I'm getting all cerebral
when you clearly need help with those high heels.
Beauty can hurt. Now you know how it feels.

John Savoie

Colors Developed by Sherwin-Williams Laboratories but Rejected by Marketing

inner-city brick

      oil plume

            menarche

fast-food gorge

      nothing quite rhymes or matches

            sunken pumpkin

lipo

      cowardice

            playstation pallor

chloroplastic

      greener than thou

            meth breath

Aryan blue

      father's little helper

            isolation

indigône

      indígoné

            hole in the ice

violence

      melanoma

            what the drowning man sees

bête noire

        night terror

                the blackness of darkness

ash cloud

        equivocation

                Alzheimer mist

blancmange

        erasure

                oblivion

Hannah Baker-Siroty

Beekeeper Outside Escanaba, Michigan

In the Upper Peninsula some bees
made a connection with a body.
The story is secondhand, from a friend
of a friend. It's not important
to be there, exactly, outside Escanaba,
to know how she took her dress off.
It was loose, light fabric, and bees were under it.
A swarm began, so she removed the only
layer, slowly, until, naked, she
scraped honey from the comb

Colin Pope

Mosquito Hawk

for Jennifer Wrisley, 1980-2010

It could've been me
asking a white waltz with my shadow
in a strange room. At the time,
I couldn't watch myself eat.
I couldn't configure a path
away from everything quick enough.
The rays of my heart split, hunting
all the little me's I wanted
to stuff inside the glass wire
of my body, legs and all.
I required return. So
I starved and died, and coiled
around my soul like a dried petal,
allowed a little wind to bully me
into the stillness whose name
I wake to each day, remembering
a life beyond living, a collection of eyes
and wings that moved forward
without apology or reason,
any way they could.

Kelly Michels

Family Portrait

My sister's skin, young, honey-veiled,
interrupted by the pale scar of her heart
that the doctors slice open every
five years since the day she was born.
She is floating on a dark ocean
where her mother drinks a bottle of wine
then another and my father runs from continent
to continent in the hidden cities of his skull.
Years from now there will be no polar bears
no glaciers, no solid ground to call home.
The years get shorter as we age and a 16 yr old
from Millbrook down the road died last night
75 in a 35 before ramming up a curb,
hitting a tree. It could have been me, 15
years ago when a judge said I was lucky
to be alive, said I should wear a football helmet
next time I get behind the wheel. My mother
is busy drinking water from a mirage while
my sister waits for her scar to turn red,
bubble with stitches, from the bubblegum
flavored anesthesia that makes her nauseous.
I wonder how many years before I have to tell her
to be careful at night, that there will always be
a man in the shadows waiting to tear you open,

to leave your body to the trees. How many more
years before I tell her I am lucky to be alive? It is
Christmas and the sky is lit in electricity, the air
sneezes raspberry and cinnamon, tinsel collects
in the corners like human hair. My father sleeps
with the windows open, the cold rattling
his bedroom door. Not frozen enough, he dreams.
Years from now there will be no more honey
on the table but enough salt to keep our arteries
awake forever. In the garage, my two brothers
erupt in a fist fight, a blizzard of arms and legs,
one brother's hand to the other's throat
waiting for god to separate them,
and I think of how we are all pelicans in winter
diving into the deep glow of the world, not knowing
where we will come back up.
I turn on the hall light for fear of disappearing,
for fear of our delicate bird voices
their votive cries, frail as a paper napkin
could somehow slip into the morning unnoticed.

Mia Ayumi Malhotra

As If

this, my wish: to be cord-
shorn, wrapped in white.

My unwashed neck's been
rung with gold. As if this

were the god whose head
I wished to crown, the one

whose hem I wished myself
beneath. He rubbed my

wound with salt, stitched
me shut like lace. My wild

tongue whistles, I'm all incisor
& skull. Ruff-bitten,

tooth-cut, I rustle in my rude
warren, pluck fur from my

belly to line my nest. We
the hunted are formed to

flee, feet furred for speed.

Elizabeth T. Gray, Jr.

Albania

On Sunday I went to Albania.
No one understood, clearly, at first, why I (or anyone) would go to Albania.
Except my father, who knew at once: "Because, before, you couldn't go to Albania."

It had never occurred to me, before, to actually go to Albania.
For years it was there, a Mars, the ultimate hole in the atlas: Albania.

Our government said you couldn't go to Albania.
Passports self-vaporized, I thought, if you went to Albania.
The Middle Ages with Missiles, over there in Albania.
And somehow also China, Albania.

But then it was suddenly Sunday, forty years later, and it was right there. I was right next to
Albania.

There's a thin strait, with small islands. You pay a ferryman to cross to Albania.
Before, people who tried to swim away were shot by men in trenches and towers guarding
Albania.

Everyone was surprised when I left, alone, for Albania.
"Given her history, were you worried when your mother went off to Albania?"
"No. Well, maybe a little," they said. "She had never mentioned Albania."

When I came back everyone asked about Albania.
They said, "What did you see in Albania?"

I began to reply but that was enough of Albania.

Perhaps it was hard for them. The idea of Albania.

Maybe they never had an Albania.

They weren't panicked. They didn't ask, "What will we do, now that we can go to Albania?"

It's been a few days now. It's as if nothing happened. As if I never went to Albania.

The chart shows two ports and several small harbors but from this far offshore there are no

lights anywhere on the coast of Albania.

As we move north, somewhere to starboard, steep and with snow, is Albania.

nominated by Beloit Poetry Journal

Theadora Siranian

Erytheia

> *As in childhood we live sweeping close to the sky and now, what dawn is this.*
> —Anne Carson

I.

My mother, a red island, a long, thin stretch
of wound: skin pulled over

bones, what's left of the flesh.
I think red like she's an island of her own,

a red-winged monster more terrible
in her physical frailty than she ever

was during my childhood, during
the days of her unpredictable madness.

II.

The body changes over time, sometimes unexpectedly:
wings sprout, scales form, the nightmares

of the mind become in reality more awful
—the romance of tragedy is replaced

by the tangible, the smell of unwashed
sheets and the wracked breathing

of a person caught not between *alive* and *dead,*
but *alive* and *dying.*

Chronic morbidity, the doctors call it, because it takes
more to kill the body off than we like to think,

because purgatory isn't allegory but a life sentence,
the poisonous bite of the counted chicken.

III.

A once-beautiful, still-dangerous woman becomes
a skeleton, raw and defenseless, lying

in a faceless place, her face placeless except
for its red, riven features. But then, even

pain, so prevalent, begins to almost lose
its magnitude here. Her body has come to define

frailty: skin thin and crimson as origami paper,
layed out on white, white.

Even the flowers look dangerous.

IV.

In a long tin house
silence, vast as a continent, grew inside

the unending buzz of summer.
Silent bedrooms and the hollow droning

of cicadas barging in like metal
shavings through the screen door.

Winter brought bitterness that peeled
cheap wallpaper and warped laminate,

silence gone as if shattered.

V.

They call it *insensible loss*, the way the moisture
leaves the body. Usually, this abandonment

occurs naturally; in more extreme instances
it's temperature change, a humid vacation

somewhere poor and beautiful makes
you sweat out that which is most precious.

I try to understand her now, especially,
in the hospital as I watch her red body

       drift in

               and out

        and in.

Tricky morphine: bouts of lucidity
are like secrets. But the only secrets

I learn are my own; my mother gives me nothing
but dreams, broken rafts made of lush,

leafy plants, a world verdant and painless.
Brilliant color without all the sharp edges.

VI.

Tonight the island lays alone on a thin sheet
thinking vaguely about loss of seasons

including *health*, and *lack of pain*, and the absence
of *pain killers*.

                She drifts in,

      she drifts out, a boat

moored by a shoddy knot.

No one has ever been able to prove to me
that the love for a loved one is a choice.

VII.

I am a spy uncovering the body,
searching the drugged, sleeping face

of my mother for artifacts of guilt,
some tiny cut-glass fragment of apology.

I am duplicitous, daughter, selfishly trying
to trade comfort for information.

Patience, desperate patience, moving me
from the bedpan to the bathroom, the clicks

and beeps in the hall and beyond limitless,
thinking about unfinished crosswords, bourbon,

the sex I don't want. The things that are mine
that she cannot have.

Jane Wong

Stemma

1.
Week, while, year. Leaves flood   in autumn.
On a curbside, a white melon rots.   Early
this morning, there was rust, rustle. A spoon in   stunted
scrub.

.

How do we return. To split, to be splitting.
A tree splits in a storm and no one   removes it
it does not drift   it does not become a boat
my purpose here   I was told
to stay whole   atoms, particles of

.

In terrible   interrogation. Sitting in a room. Waiting.
A bee circles, smelling my hair.   A tree blooms
in white, but I can not see.

.

Night.   A bird stands on one leg.
Others follow. They collapse wings.   Sweet arrest
this mass   sleeping
I will be sleeping soon.

.

Pace, past, point. A century passes through my hands
I open my hands to see   ocean. Mutiny, mute,
I rest where I do not   belong

.

To bend   in stillness, to ease in   wind.
A lake curves around a road. In rain, everything changes.
Half of nothing is nothing. A water jar tips over and
sigh

.

Echo and   release. Weak, weakened   a crab thrown in water
spared.   I am thankful.   The thin claws wrapped around
my finger   in need of brightness
in need of   breakage

.

Span. Spell. Stretch.   I sail across ocean
a great division   rising in crests
miniature boats pass me by   carrying no one

.

A fish in a deep pan, skeletal.   All things are the result of time.
Brooms splinter with wear. I left a plant   to die
I am no master   floating to and
fro

2.

A pear tree   falls   not because of disease but because of
necessity. Beetles fill the tree   silently. It will disappear

.

Trouble no trouble here.   City officials took my father away today
They used sticks, not guns   sticks seem worse
You can hit an ox with a stick for a long time.   I watched him hit an ox once
he kept going   it wouldn't move

.

This morning, a beetle crawled out of a pear   thin legs sticking in
grit. It bit where it hurt   my mouth the very center of it—
I couldn't even shout

.

Two birds   eclipse. The sky has no alarm, just   expanse.
I go visit my father   I am five and he is
weeping   head against the wall.
The guards finish their soup   bowls packed tightly like halved onions.
Everything I want to say   no longer exists.
I can't even see   his face.
Shroud, shadow. A mirror shines   somewhere else

3.

Whist, whistle. A bird cries across   a road, turning into
dusk. Dusk covers the lake with trees.
Where leaves fall and where leaves   won't. I gather in
the won't

.

Wading through mud, I find a frog   a sick, stuck frog
I bury it in a jar.   To keep what
we can not. The humming throat kicking   dirt under water

.

My father sleeps on the cell floor   how a small animal sleeps, never quite
there. A light shines on his crown   his thin black hair in white gossamer, glint

.

A bird in treble.
For what   it matters, I can't stand
still, troubled

No trouble here no   water in
the jar. The frog dies and I go and open a map   to place it. I name
every city, town, except ours. Places exist in time. Palenque, Pompeii. I float through
no matter
remnant of air, atom   thrown

.

I sleep through a future
through the time of ants   I wake when they don't exist.
Everything is affected: no spiders, no leaves, no trees to speak of   my father disappears
in a hollow. The guards search for him   but they can not tell the difference
between night and day. I'm afraid

I made this happen

this world waiting for something to arrive
a queen, a cry, a jar for what—   I need to believe

it is beyond me

nominated by Asian American Poetry Retreat

Terry Lucas

Break

    After Kim Addonizio

It feels so good to break a rack of pool balls,
to stand with your legs apart, stroking the cue
between fingers and thumb, aiming at the tight
diamond, then thrusting your pelvis into an explosion
of red and purple and blue—it feels good
to move in on the cue, chalk up your stick,
pound the first ball into the corner pocket
with enough draw to get shape for the next shot.
Then another and another, and you no longer wonder
why some real cool boys skipped school,
how they ended up dead so soon. You can feel them
in your body—the breaking sounds around the room
like the splintering of bones, the firing of Berettas
and Glocks, the jukebox wailing like mothers and fathers.
And now you want to smash every cue in the house,
rip the green felt off each slab of slate,
take a hammer to the balls, a hatchet
to the whorled grain table legs, douse the place
with gasoline and strike a match, watch the smoke
rise through the bright, silent sky—so high
that nothing can reach it. But you fear

the cloud would rain down as ash,
feed trees to harvest for more pool halls.
So you stand there knocking in balls,
until your stick feels light, innocent.
Then you rack them up again.

Chris Tanseer

Appalachian Homecoming

A dinner bell reverberates through the valley,
Appalachian slow-going blues, the leaves dance shadows
                              on the forest floor
And through my thoughts

As if each were inseparable from the other.
I'm at it again, rationing out my ration to the cedars and loons.
Wanderlust in the loose veil of sundown.

Returning to you seems easy
                              outside the thing, like watching
An osprey above the tree line swoop low, spear the water
And talon a trout. I've known men who have lived

In the gaps of syllables, wed
The evenings outside the lit window of a former lover—intimate now
With a whiff from the bedroom fan, or the familiar voice

Of a distant body, a syllable astray. *Syllable*, from
The Greek *syl-*, "together with," and *lab-*, "to take."
Miles are the easiest distance to transverse.

Odysseus reached Penelope
In just ten years. Which is why, after
Nobody escaped from Polyphemus and, when

Nobody revealed his name, it lived to haunt
                    the blind hermit. Syllables astray.
Words lack alone. I've known men who've waited lifetimes
In the next room.

Anders Carlson-Wee

Northern Corn

Traveling alone through Minnesota as the corn
comes in. Steel silos filling to the brim.
Black trees leaning off the south sides of hills
as the cold light falls slantwise against
the gristmills. You have allowed another year
to pass. You have learned very little. But that little
is what you are throwing in the furnace.
That little is stoking the dust-coals of last year
and burning something. Burning blue.
The ninety-year-old father is bringing
his crop in. He climbs off the thresher, checks
the engine, moves an oak branch. He pours
rye whiskey from a thermos and sips
the lidless excess of his private noon.
The size of his hands. The size of one finger.
The flathead prairie of his calloused thumb-pad.
He lies awake in the middle of the night
and whispers something and suddenly loves
his son again. The way excess falls
through him. The way oil runs down
the Mississippi River and remains on the surface
and burns. The father no longer breathing.
The respirator breathing. The father lying

in a hospital bed in a nightgown.
The plastic tubes and machinery. The whole
hospital breathing. The fluorescent lights
breathing. The janitor waxing the white-tile
floors at midnight while life is trying hard
to leave. You must go to your father
while he is still your father. You must hold
him. You must kiss him. You must listen.
You must see the son in the father and wonder.
You must admit that you wonder. Stand above
him and wonder. Drop his swelled-up hand.
Whisper something. Now unplug the machine.

Patrick Haas

Oxen on the Last Day

they will follow their heads down
knowing they will
never rise again, dreaming
they are mountains, eyes
jetting left to right to left
like boustrophedonic clocks
hung inside vacant rooms

as hoof tracks
in the mud fill with mud

and we'll shew the past
from our minds
brushing
shadows away
with light, keeping
the no-time of toil
like they used to

bodies shellacked
with waiting for the sky
to give up giving itself

away for night to swing
displaced around their horns
for rain to slurry along

their enormous spines
for the fabulist wind to lead us
down, to lead us

like lanterns through the fields

Martin Arnold

Until Bullets Turn to Rain Against Your Flesh

If you want to know what it means to be American,
Take acting classes.

If you want to know how to be a good actor,
Spend your summer playing Geronimo at a theme park,

Honing your stare against your family's slaughtered bodies
Until bullets turn to rain against your flesh.

Geronimo could stop time
So some shifts feel like they never end,

But with practice you'll see your house pillaged
In the pity of a child's stare.

Don't speak Spanish. It confuses the audience.
Say Apache not Chiricahua or Bedonkohe

Because visitors can't see the sacred in stealing horses.
Unlike the governments of Sonora, Chihuahua, and Durango

Who into the late 19th century still paid up to $300
For an Apache scalp, this apprenticeship pays minimum wage.

If you return next summer, you'll have lived long enough
To regret whatever dignity you surrendered to General Miles

Under terms Cleveland won't honor. For each day's finale,
Teddy Roosevelt will parade you, his captured savage,

Down the streets of Washington, Roosevelt, the hunter, who said
Man is the most dangerous animal.

Christopher Nelson

Fidelity

Night comes first to the innermost
branches of the elm, then hedgerows, then entire lawns.

My neighbor gets ready for bed, her one lit window and the red pulse

of a radio tower above the bay. Our backyards are small
and touch each other along one side.

nominated by the University of Arizona

Contributors' Notes

TORY ADKISSON grew up in the California High Desert between the San Bernardino and San Gabriel Mountains. His poems have appeared or are forthcoming in *32 Poems, Linebreak, Copper Nickel, Third Coast, Barrow Street*, and elsewhere. A graduate of the MFA program at The Ohio State University, he is currently a doctoral student in creative writing at the University of Georgia.

MARTIN ARNOLD holds an MFA from the University of North Carolina at Greensboro and teaches at Guilford College. He is the associate poetry editor of *storySouth*. His poetry has been published in *Verse Daily, Denver Quarterly, Crab Orchard Review, the Carolina Quarterly*, and elsewhere. His chapbook, *A Million Distant Glittering Catastrophes*, won the 2009-2010 Pavement Saw Chapbook Competition.

HANNAH BAKER-SIROTY was born in Newton, Massachusetts, and currently lives with her wife in Arlington. She has studied writing at the University of Wisconsin-Madison, Trinity College-Dublin, and Sarah Lawrence College. A former poetry fellow at The Writers' Room of Boston and resident at the Vermont Studio Center, she was recently a featured reader in the Boston's Best U35 Reading Series. Hannah teaches writing at Pine Manor College and is working on her second book of poems—about vice-presidents. Her first book, *Odd of the Ordinary*, is awaiting publication. You can find out more about Hannah at poetrying.com.

HARRY BAULD is from Medford, Massachusetts. His poems have appeared in, among others, *Nimrod, Southern Poetry Review, The Southeast Review, Verse Daily, Ruminate, The Baltimore Review, Whiskey Island*, and *Deliberately Thirsty* (UK). In 2008 he won the New Millenium Writings poetry prize. He has taught and coached baseball, basketball, and boxing at high schools in Vermont and New York and currently lives and teaches in the Bronx.

REBECCA BAUMAN was born in Texas and raised in Missouri and Florida. Much of her undergraduate career was funded by work in wildlife rehabilitation, outreach, and education. In 2007, she was employed as an editorial intern and produced freelance content for *Esquire*. She is now pursuing her MFA in Creative Writing with an emphasis in poetry at the University of Florida. In turn, Bauman teaches various writing classes at the school, and won the 2012 Calvin A. VanderWerf Award for university-wide excellence in graduate teaching. She is the first student from the university's creative writing program to receive this honor.

OLIVER BENDORF grew up in Iowa City, Iowa, and is now an MFA candidate at the University of Wisconsin-Madison, where he edits *Devil's Lake*. His poems have appeared or are forthcoming in *Ninth Letter, Anti-, The Journal, PANK, Quarterly West*, in an anthology of transgender poets, and elsewhere. A Lambda Literary Fellow in Poetry, Oliver is also a finalist for the 2012 Ruth Lilly Poetry Fellowship.

SEAN BISHOP's poems have appeared or are forthcoming in *Boston Review, Crazyhorse, Harvard Review, Indiana Review, jubilat, Ploughshares, Poetry*, and elsewhere. He teaches in the MFA program at the University of Wisconsin. He is also the founding editor of *Better: Culture & Lit* (bettermagazine.org).

SHEVAUN BRANNIGAN is an MFA candidate at Bennington College and a graduate of The Jiménez-Porter Writers' House at the University of Maryland. She has been previously published in *Lumina, So to Speak,* and *CALYX*, as well as other journals. Additional works can be found at shevaunbrannigan. wordpress.com. Shevaun is also an animal rights activist, and operates a fundraising site for special needs guinea pigs at sponsoraguineapig.blogspot. com.

CHUCK CARLISE was born in Canton, Ohio, on the first Flag Day of the Jimmy Carter Era and has lived in a dozen states and two continents since. He is the author of the chapbooks *A Broken Escalator Still Isn't the Stairs* (Concrete Wolf, 2011) and *Casual Insomniac* (Bateau, 2011). He recently completed his PhD in Literature and Creative Writing at the University of Houston, where he was the 2012 InPrint/Paul Verlaine Poetry Prize winner and the nonfiction editor for *Gulf Coast*. His own poems and essays appear in *Southern Review, Pleiades, DIAGRAM, Quarterly West*, and elsewhere. More info on Chuck can be found at chuckcarlise.com.

ANDERS CARLSON-WEE grew up in Moorhead, Minnesota and at 15 moved to Minneapolis where he became a professional rollerblader. After high school he lived in the Cascade Mountains of Washington State for two years before attending Fairhaven College in Bellingham. At Fairhaven he studied with the poet Mary Cornish and designed his own degree in creative writing. Anders has found much of his inspiration to write from his travels throughout the United States by bicycle and freight train. He is currently in Greece on a half-year walk through the Balkans.

AVIVA ENGLANDER CRISTY is a doctoral candidate in English at the University of Wisconsin-Milwaukee, where she serves as a poetry editor for *the cream city* *review*. Her chapbook, *The Interior Structure*, is forthcoming from dancing girl press. Aviva received her MFA in poetry from George Mason University. Her poems have appeared in or are forthcoming from *So To Speak, The Hollins Critic, BlazeVox, decomP magazine*, and *The Chiron Review*, among others.

ERIN GANAWAY holds a Master of Fine Arts from Hollins University. Her work has appeared or is forthcoming in the *New York Quarterly, Third Coast, Sea Stories*, and elsewhere. She was a featured poet in *Town Creek Poetry*, and her poems were selected for inclusion in the Georgia volume of *The Southern Poetry Anthology*. She divides her time between Atlanta and Cape Cod.

ELIZABETH T. GRAY, JR. is a poet, translator, and corporate consultant. Her translations of Iran's major mystical poet, Hafiz-i Shirazi (d. 1389) were published by White Cloud Press in 1995. Poems and translations (from Persian and Tibetan) have appeared or are forthcoming in *The Kenyon Review, Beloit Poetry Journal, The Harvard Review, The Cimarron Review, Poetry International, Ploughshares, Agni, The New Orleans Review, The New Haven Review, Mantis*, and *Provincetown Arts*. She has a JD from Harvard Law School and an MFA from Warren Wilson College. She lives in New York City. elizabethtgrayjr.com.

SARAH GREEN is a PhD candidate in Creative Writing at Ohio University. Her poems have appeared in *Gettysburg Review, FIELD, Mid-American Review, Redivider, H-ngm-n, Forklift Ohio, Cortland Review*, and other magazines. She is the recipient of a 2009 Pushcart Prize. She co-founded and co-edits the writer-musician magazine *Octave*; her first record, "Climb," with the band Heartacre came out in 2011. She lives in Athens, Ohio.

PATRICK HAAS received his MA in Writing from Portland State University. His work has appeared or is forthcoming in *Salt Hill, Unstuck, Anomalous Press, Dark Sky*, and *Petri Press*.

JENNY GROPP HESS's writing resides in *Seneca Review, Seattle Review, Colorado Review, American Letters & Commentary, DIAGRAM, Typo,* and others. She is a past winner of the *Columbia: A Journal of Literature and Art* poetry contest and *Unsaid's* Ivory-Billed Woodpecker Award for Fiction in the Face of Adversity. The former editor of *Black Warrior Review*, she is now managing editor at *The Georgia Review*.

BRADLEY HARRISON grew up in small-town Iowa and is a graduate of Truman State University. Currently a Michener Fellow at the University of Texas in Austin, his work can be found in *Gulf Coast, CutBank, The Los Angeles Review, Hunger Mountain, New Orleans Review,* and other journals. His chapbook *Diorama of a People, Burning* is available from Ricochet Editions (2012).

LEXA HILLYER received her MFA in poetry from Stonecoast at the University of Southern Maine. Her first book, *Acquainted with the Cold* (Bona Fide Books, 2012) won the 2011 Melissa Lanitis Gregory Poetry Prize. She also won the Inaugural Poetry Prize from *Tusculum Review* and First Prize in Poetry from *Brick & Mortar Review*. Lexa edited at Harper Collins and Penguin, and now runs Paper Lantern Lit.

PAUL HLAVA is a poet and English teacher. He has been published in *Gulf Coast, Agriculture Reader,* and *Rattle*, among others. His poems have been performed at New York's Dixon Place theater and Bowery Poetry Club. He lives in Brooklyn.

KASANDRA LARSEN's chapbook, *Stellar Telegram*, won the 2009 Sheltering Pines Press Chapbook Competition. One of three winners of the Third Wednesday

2011 Poetry Contest, she has been twice nominated for a Pushcart Prize. She's also been twice nominated for a Best of the Net Award, and was a finalist in the Tiferet 2010 Sacred Poetry Contest judged by Marie Howe. Her work has appeared in journals in the U.S., Canada, and the U.K., including: *100 Poets Against the War, The Advocate, Amethyst Arsenic, Babylon Burning: 9/11 Five Years On, Ballard Street Poetry Journal, Blood Lotus, Bloodroot Literary Magazine, Blue Earth Review, Breakwater Review, Denver Syntax, ellipsis, Essence Poetry, Freshwater, Full of Crow, Hawai'i Pacific Review, Moondance, The Moose & Pussy, The Nervous Breakdown, The November 3rd Club, nthposition, Osprey Journal, Poems-for-All, Pure Francis, Roanoke Review, Short Fuse: The Global Anthology of New Fusion Poetry, SLAB, Swamp Lily Review, tinfoildresses, Two Hawks Quarterly, White Pelican Review, Work to a Calm,* and *The Write Room.* Originally from Boston, she moved to New Orleans in 2000.

TERRY LUCAS grew up in New Mexico and has lived in the San Francisco bay area for over a decade. Four times nominated for a Pushcart Prize, his poems have appeared in *Green Mountains Review, Columbia Poetry Review,* and *Fifth Wednesday Journal,* among others. Terry has recent or forthcoming work in *Great River Review, Sin Fronteras/Writers Without Borders, The Citron Review, MiPOesias,* and *A Clean, Well-Lighted Place.* His chapbook, *Making Up The Dead,* was selected by Dorianne Laux for second prize in the 2010 Palettes & Quills Chapbook Contest. Terry is a 2008 Poetry MFA graduate of New England College and an associate editor for Trio House Press.

CATE LYCURGUS grew up south of San Francisco and is currently pursuing her MFA at Indiana University, where she served as poetry editor for *Indiana Review.*

MIA AYUMI MALHOTRA is the associate editor of *Lantern Review: A Journal of Asian American Poetry.* She holds an MFA from the University of Washington, and her poems are featured and forthcoming in *DIAGRAM, Asian American Literary Review, diode,* and others. She currently lives and teaches in the San Francisco Bay Area.

VICTORIA LYNNE MCCOY holds an MFA in poetry from Sarah Lawrence College. Her work has appeared in *Boxcar Poetry Review, Used Furniture Review, PANK,* and *Union Station Magazine,* among others. A member of the louderARTS Project, Victoria lives in Brooklyn and works for Four Way Books.

JANET MCNALLY's poetry and fiction has appeared or is forthcoming in *Hayden's Ferry Review, Crazyhorse, Gettysburg Review, Mid-American Review, Ecotone, Crab Orchard Review,* and others. She is a graduate of the University of Notre Dame's MFA program, and in 2008 she was awarded a fellowship in fiction by the New York Foundation for the Arts. She teaches creative writing at Canisius College in Buffalo, New York.

DANIEL MELTZ is a technical writer at Google. As a younger man he taught geometry to the deaf and WordPerfect to the blind. He lives in midtown Manhattan between a beauty parlor and a nail salon. His work has been published in *American Poetry Review, upstreet, Mudfish, Audio Zine, Assisi, Temenos, FortyOunceBachelors,* and *CrossConnect.*

KELLY MICHELS holds an MFA from North Carolina State University where she also won the Academy of American Poets Prize. Her poetry has been featured in *Nimrod, Mad Poet's Review, Blue Fifth Review, Ruminate,* and *From the Depths,* among others. She lives in Raleigh, North Carolina. For more information, please see kellymichels.com.

MEGGIE MONAHAN received her MFA in poetry from the University of Houston where she served as nonfiction editor for *Gulf Coast*. Her work has appeared or is forthcoming in *Mid-American Review, Third Coast, Ruminate, Sonora Review*, and elsewhere. Meggie currently lives in Houston where she works as a private editor and eats (too many?) breakfast tacos. She is very grateful for the opportunity to appear in this anthology.

JENNIFER MOORE has poems published or forthcoming in *Barrow Street, Hayden's Ferry Review, Handsome, Columbia Poetry Review* and elsewhere, and criticism in *Jacket2* and *The Offending Adam*. She holds degrees from the University of Colorado and the University of Illinois at Chicago, and is an assistant professor of creative writing at Ohio Northern University.

CHRISTOPHER NELSON is the author of *Blue House*, published in the New American Poets Chapbook Series (PSA, 2009). He studied creative writing at Southern Utah University and the University of Arizona, where he was a Jacob K. Javits Fellow. His interviews with poets can be read online at *Under A Warm Green Linden*.

MATTHEW NIENOW is the author of three chapbooks, including *The End of the Folded Map* (Codhill Press, 2011). His poems have appeared or are forthcoming in *AGNI, Beloit Poetry Journal, New England Review, Poetry, Southwest Review*, and many other magazines and anthologies (among them *Best New Poets 2007*). His honors include fellowships from the National Endowment for the Arts, the Bread Loaf Writers' Conference, the Elizabeth George Foundation, and Artist Trust. He lives in Port Townsend, Washington, with his wife and two sons, where he works as a boatbuilder.

JEFF OAKS's newest chapbook of poems, *Mistakes with Strangers*, will be published by Seven Kitchens Press in 2012. His poems have appeared most recently in *FIELD, Poemeleon, Bloom, Court Green*, and *Zocalo Public Square*. He teaches writing at the University of Pittsburgh.

ALLYSON PATY is the author of a chapbook, *The Further Away* ([Sic] Detroit, 2012). Her poems can be found in *Tin House, Gulf Coast, DIAGRAM, Colorado Review, Denver Quarterly, Harpur Palate, Handsome, Sixth Finch*, and elsewhere. She is from New York, where she is co-editor of Singing Saw Press.

COLIN POPE's poetry has appeared or is forthcoming in *Slate, The New York Quarterly, Texas Review, Linebreak*, and *The Los Angeles Review*, among others. He was the 2011-12 Clark Writer-in-Residence at Texas State University, where he teaches in the English Department. He is currently poetry editor at *Southwestern American Literature* and was formerly the poetry editor at *Front Porch Journal*. "Mosquito Hawk" is about Jennie Wrisley, a beautiful poet who ended her life far too soon.

MICHELE POULOS is the author of the forthcoming chapbook *A Disturbance in the Air*, which won the 2012 Slapering Hol Press Chapbook Competition. Her poems and fiction have appeared in *The Southern Review, Crab Orchard Review, Copper Nickel, Sycamore Review, The Southern Poetry Anthology*, and elsewhere. She is currently a student in the MFA in Creative Writing program at Arizona State University.

MEGHAN PRIVITELLO is a poet living in New Jersey. Her work has appeared or is forthcoming in *NOÖ Journal, Gigantic Sequins, Phantom Limb, Sixth Finch, Redivider, The New Megaphone*, & *Barn Owl Review*. You can follow her on twitter @meghanpriv.

BEN PURKERT's poems have recently appeared or are forthcoming in *The New Yorker, Fence, Denver Quarterly, The Awl, DIAGRAM, New Orleans Review, Carolina Quarterly, Spoon River Poetry Review,* and elsewhere. He holds an MFA from NYU and is currently completing his first poetry manuscript, *One Good*. He is also Poetry Editor of *Bodega* (bodegamag.com).

MICHAEL ROCHE has a bachelor's degree from the College of the Holy Cross in Worcester, Massachussetts and is currently pursuing his MFA at Virginia Tech, where he teaches composition. He is also a reader and blog contributor for *the minnesota review*.

MARTIN ROCK is a poet, editor, and web designer living in Brooklyn. His poems have appeared in *Black Warrior Review, Conduit, DIAGRAM, Salamander,* and other journals. His collaborative chapbook with Phillip D. Ischy, *Fish, You Bird*, was published by Pilot Books. He is editor in chief of *Loaded Bicycle* and managing editor of *Epiphany, a Literary Journal*, where he makes letterpress chapbooks for Epiphany Editions. He holds an MFA from New York University.

Though young at heart, old in soul, **JOHN SAVOIE** is nonetheless amused to come so late to be this New. Long ago his poetry won two Hopwood Awards at the University of Michigan. More recently his poems have appeared in *Poetry, JAMA,* and *Shenandoah*. Having studied at Notre Dame and Yale he currently teaches great books at Southern Illinois University Edwardsville.

MICHAEL MARTIN SHEA is an MFA candidate and John and Renée Grisham Fellow at the University of Mississippi, where he edits *Yalobusha Review*. His poems have previously appeared or are forthcoming in *Ninth Letter, Salt Hill, The Journal, Sycamore Review, Hayden's Ferry Review*, and elsewhere.

Theadora Siranian is an MFA Poetry candidate at the University of Massachusetts, Boston. She has been published or has poems forthcoming in *Gigantic Sequins, mojo, elimae*, and *DIAGRAM*. In 2007 she received the Academy of American Poets Prize from Emerson College.

Sophia G. Starmack received an MA in French and Francophone Literature from Bryn Mawr College and is currently completing an MFA in Poetry at Sarah Lawrence College. She works as a writing teacher and tutor in New York City.

Christine Stroik Stocke is a graduate of the master's program in English at the University of Wisconsin-Milwaukee. She and her husband recently moved to another land of beer and cheese: Holland. Other works by Christine can be found in *Word, Rio Grande Review, Menu 971, WI People* and *Ideas*, and the 2013 WI Poets' Calendar.

Originally from North Carolina, **Chris Tanseer** currently lives in the (disconcertingly green) desert of Salt Lake City, where he is a PhD candidate at the University of Utah in Literature & Creative Writing, and a reader for *Sugar House Review*. He received an MFA in poetry from George Mason University in 2007. His work has appeared in such places as journals, his trashcan, and on quite a number of refrigerators. If you're bored… christanseer.com.

Gale Marie Thompson's first collection of poems, *Soldier On*, is forthcoming from Tupelo Press. Her work has appeared in the *Denver Quarterly, Columbia: A Journal of Literature and Art, Volt, Salt Hill*, and others. She is a recent graduate of the University of Massachusetts MFA Program and is a PhD candidate at the University of Georgia. She is creator and editor of *Jellyfish Magazine*.

COREY VAN LANDINGHAM recently completed her MFA at Purdue University, where she was a Poetry Editor for *Sycamore Review*. She has won the *Indiana Review* 1/2 K Prize, the 2012 AWP Intro Journals Award, an Academy of American Poets University Prize, and has been awarded two Bread Loaf Work-Study Scholarships. Her poems have appeared or are forthcoming in *Colorado Review, Crazyhorse, Cream City Review, Hayden's Ferry Review, Indiana Review, Mid-American Review, The Southern Review, Third Coast, West Branch*, and elsewhere.

TIMOTHY DANIEL WELCH has a BA in music composition from Santa Clara University, an MFA in Poetry from San Diego State University, and a PhD in English at Florida State University. He has a ferocity for California, music, and painting the occasional nude. As his strange and imagistic poetry attests, he has never met an adjective he didn't like.

ROSS WHITE is the editor of *Inch*, a tiny magazine featuring short poems and microfiction. His work has appeared in *New England Review, Poetry Daily, Salon.com, The Collagist, Greensboro Review*, and others. With Matthew Olzmann, he edited *Another & Another: An Anthology from the Grind Daily Writing Series* (Bull City Press, 2012), which collects the work of 47 emerging and established poets. He teaches poetry at the University of North Carolina at Chapel Hill and the North Carolina School of Science and Mathematics.

JANE WONG received her MFA from the Iowa Writers' Workshop and is a former U.S. Fulbright Fellow. She is also the recipient of scholarships to the Bread Loaf Writers' Conference and the Fine Arts Work Center in Provincetown. Her poems have appeared in *CutBank, ZYZZYVA, Mid-American Review, Octopus, The Journal, EOAGH*, and others. She lives in Seattle.

Acknowledgments

Tory Adkisson's "Homosexuality" was previously published in *Colorado Review*.

Oliver Bendorf's "I Promised Her My Hands Wouldn't Get Any Larger" was previously published in *Ninth Letter*.

Sean Bishop's "Black Hole Owners Association" was previously published in *Alaska Quarterly Review*.

Erin Ganaway's "Meds" was previously published in *Third Coast*.

Elizabeth T. Gray, Jr.'s "Albania" was previously published in *Beloit Poetry Journal*.

Patrick Haas's "Oxen on the Last Day" was previously published in *Salt Hill*.

Jenny Gropp Hess's "Months After the Crash, the Blind Aerobatic Pilot Speaks" was previously published in *Beecher's Magazine*.

Terry Lucas's "Break" was previously published in *PoetsArtists*.

Mia Ayumi Malhotra's "As If" was previously published in *The Monarch Review*.

Victoria Lynne McCoy's "Self-Portrait in Unfinished Letters" was previously published in *Used Furniture Review*.

Janet McNally's "Maggie Leaves the Underworld" was previously published in *Hayden's Ferry Review*.

Daniel Meltz's "Intrinsic Marimbas" was previously published in *upstreet*.

Jennifer Moore's "As a Debutante I Adjusted My Hatpin" was previously published in *Puerto Del Sol*.

Christopher Nelson's "Fidelity" was previously published by The University of Arizona Poetry Center.

Matthew Nienow's "O Anchor" was previously published in *Beloit Poetry Journal*.

Jeff Oaks's "Saint Wrench" was previously published in *Poemeleon*.

Allyson Paty's "Score for the New Cotillion" was previously published in *Sixth Finch*.

Colin Pope's "Mosquito Hawk" was previously published in *Grist: The Journal for Writers*.

Michael Martin Shea's "Rough Draft of a Poem About Heartbeats" was previously published in *Epiphany*.

Corey Van Landingham's "Tabernacle for an Adolescence" was previously published in *Third Coast*.

Jane Wong's "Stemma" was previously published in *Dear Sir*.

Participating Magazines

32 Poems Magazine
P.O. Box 383
Earlville, NY 13332
32poems.com

AGNI
Boston University
236 Bay State Road
Boston, MA 02215
bu.edu/agni

Anti-
4237 Beethoven Avenue
St. Louis, MO 63116
anti-poetry.com

The Antioch Review
Antioch College
P.O. Box 148
Yellow Springs, OH 45387
antiochreview.org

Arsenic Lobster
1830 W 18Th St
Chicago, IL 60608
arseniclobster.magere.com

*Bamboo Ridge: Journal of Hawaii
Literature and Arts*
P.O. Box 61781
Honolulu, HI 96839-1781
bambooridge.com

Bat City Review
The University of Texas at Austin
Department of English, The
University of Texas at Austin
1 University Station B5000
Austin, TX 78712
batcityreview.com

The Believer
849 Valencia St.
San Francisco, CA 94110
believermag.com

Bellevue Literary Review
NYU School of Medicine
Department of Medicine
550 First Avenue, OBV-A612
New York, NY 10016
BLReview.org

Bellingham Review
Western Washington University
MS-9053
Bellingham, WA 98225
bhreview.org

Beloit Poetry Journal
The Beloit Poetry Journal Foundation,
Inc.
P.O. Box 151
Farmington, ME 04938
bpj.org

Birmingham Poetry Review
UAB, HB203, 1530 3rd Ave S
Birmingham, Al 35294
birminghampoetryreview.org

The Bitter Oleander Press
4983 Tall Oaks Drive
Fayetteville, NY 13066-9776
bitteroleander.com

Black Warrior Review
University of Alabama
Box 862936
Tuscaloosa, AL 35486
bwr.ua.edu

Blackbird
Virginia Commonwealth University
Department of English
P.O. Box 843082
Richmond, VA 23284-3082
blackbird.vcu.edu

Blood Orange Review
1495 Evergreen Ave NE
Salem, OR 97301
bloodorangereview.com

Boston Review
35 Medford St.
P.O. Box 425786
Cambridge, MA 02142
bostonreview.net

Boxcar Poetry Review
630 S. Kenmore Ave, Apt 206
Los Angeles, CA 90005
boxcarpoetry.com

The Carolina Quarterly
The University of North Carolina
Greenlaw Hall CB#3520
Chapel Hill, NC 27599-3520

Cave Wall
P.O. Box 29546
Greensboro, NC 27429-9546
cavewallpress.com

Cerise Press
P.O. Box 241187
Omaha, NE 68124
cerisepress.com

Cincinnati Review
University of Cincinnati
P.O. Box 210069
Cincinnati, OH 45221
cincinnatireview.com

Collagist
Dzanc Books
1334 Woodbourne Street
Westland, MI 48186
dzancbooks.org/the-collagist

Colorado Review
Colorado State University
The Center for Literary Publishing
9105 Campus Delivery / Dept. of
English
Fort Collins, CO 80523-9105
coloradoreview.colostate.edu

The Common
Amherst College
Frost Library, Amherst College
Amherst, MA 01002
thecommononline.org

Contrary
P.O. Box 806363
Chicago, IL 60680
contrarymagazine.com

*The Dead Mule School of Southern
Literature*
Second Street
Washington, NC 27889
helenl.wordpress.com

*FIELD: Contemporary Poetry and
Poetics*
Oberlin College Press
50 North Professor Street
Oberlin, OH 44074
oberlin.edu/ocpress

Fjords
2932 B Langhorne Rd
Lynchburg, VA 24501
fjordsreview.com

Florida Review
University of Central Florida
English Department
P.O. Box 161400
Orlando, FL 32816-1400
flreview.com

The Gettysburg Review
Gettysburg College
300 N. Washington Street
Gettysburg, PA 17325-1491
gettysburgreview.com

Gold Wake Press
5108 Avalon Drive
Randolph, MA 02368
goldwakepress.org

The Greensboro Review
University of North Carolina,
Greensboro
MFA Writing Program
3302 Moore Humanities and
Research Admin. Bldg.
Greensboro, NC 27402-6170
greensbororeview.org

Guernica
395 Fort Washington Ave., Apt. 57
New York, NY 10033
guernicamag.com

Hayden's Ferry Review
Arizona State University
The Virginia G. Piper Center for
Creative Writing
P.O. Box 875002
Tempe, AZ 85287-5002
haydensferryreview.org

I M A G E
3307 Third Avenue West
Seattle, WA 98119
imagejournal.org

In Posse Review
Web Del Sol / Michael Neff
30 Rock Ridge Road
Fairfax, CA 94930
inpossereview.com

Indiana Review
Indiana University
Ballantine Hall 465
1020 E. Kirkwood Ave.
Bloomington, IN 47405-7103
indianareview.org

The Iowa Review
University of Iowa
308 EPB
Iowa City, IA 52242-1408
iowareview.org

Juked
17149 Flanders St.
Los Angeles, CA 91344
juked.com

The Kenyon Review
Kenyon College
Finn House
102 W Wiggin St.
Gambier, OH 43022-9623
kenyonreview.org

Ledge Magazine
40 Maple Avenue
Bellport, NY 11713
theledgemagazine.com

The Los Angeles Review
Red Hen Press
P.O. Box 2458
Redmond, WA 98073
losangelesreview.org

The MacGuffin
Schoolcraft College
18600 Haggerty Road
Livonia, MI 48152
macguffin.org

Mayday
New American Press
2606 E. Locust St.
Milwaukee, WI 53211
MAYDAYMagazine.com

Memorious: A Journal of New Verse and Fiction
memorious.org
Somerville, MA 02144

Michigan Quarterly Review
University of Michigan
0576 Rackham Bldg.
915 East Washington St.
Ann Arbor, MI 48019-1070
michiganquarterlyreview.com

The Missouri Review
University of Missouri
357 McReynolds Hall
Columbia, MO 65211
missourireview.com

New Guard Review
P.O. Box 10612
Portland, ME 04104
newguardreview.com

New Letters
University of Missouri-Kansas City
5101 Rockhill Road
Kansas City, MO 64110
newletters.org

Ninth Letter
234 English, Univ. of Illinois
608 S. Wright St.
Urbana, IL 61801
ninthletter.com

Outrider Press
2036 N Winds Drive
Dyer, IN 46311

Pank
Michigan Tech
1400 Townsend Dr.
Department of Humanities
Houghton, MI 49931
pankmagazine.com

Ploughshares
Emerson College
120 Boylston St.
Boston, MA 02116
pshares.org

Poemeleon: A Journal of Poetry
poemeleon.org

Quiddity
1500 North Fifth Street
Springfield, IL 62702
quiddity.ben.edu

Rattle
12411 Ventura Blvd
Studio City, CA 91604
rattle.com

River Styx
Big River Association
3547 Olive Street Suite 107
Saint Louis, MO 63103
riverstyx.org

Salamander
Suffolk University English
Department
41 Temple Street
Boston, MA 02114
salamandermag.org

Sentence
Firewheel Editions
firewheel-editions.org

*So to Speak: a feminist journal of
language and art*
George Mason University
4400 University Drive, MSN 2C5
Fairfax, VA 22030-4444
sotospeakjournal.org

Sou'wester
Southern Illinois University
Department of English Language &
Literature
Box 1438
Edwardsville, IL 62026-1438
siue.edu/ENGLISH/SW

The Southeast Review
Florida State University
English Department
Tallahassee, FL 32306
southeastreview.org

Southern Indiana Review
University of Southern Indiana
Orr Center #2009
8600 University Boulevard
Evansville, IN 47712
southernindianareview.org

The Southern Review
Louisiana State University
3990 W. Lakeshore Drive
Baton Rouge, LA 70808
lsu.edu/thesouthernreview

Spillway
Tebot Bach
P.O. Box 7887
Huntington Beach, CA 92615
tebotbach.org/spillway.html

St. Petersburg Review
Box 2888
Concord, NH 03302
stpetersburgreview.com

Stirring : A Literary Collection
Sundress Publications
114 Newridge Rd
Oak Ridge, TN 37830
sundresspublications.com/stirring

Subtropics
English Dept. P.O. Box 112075
University of Florida
Gainesville, FL 32611
english.ufl.edu/subtropics

Sycamore Review
Purdue University
Department of English
500 Oval Drive
West Lafayette, IN 47907-2038
sycamorereview.com

Tar River Poetry
East Carolina University
113 Erwin Hall
Mail Stop 159
Greenville, NC 27858
tarriverpoetry.com

The Tusculum Review
Tusculum College
60 Shiloh RD
P.O. Box 5113
Greeneville, TN 37743
tusculum.edu/tusculumreview

upstreet, a literary magazine
P. O. Box 105
Richmond, MA 01254-0105
upstreet-mag.org

Unsplendid
c/o Douglas Basford
169 Mariner St., Apt. 2
Buffalo, NY 14201
unsplendid.com

Waccamaw
Department of English
Coastal Carolina University
Conway, SC 29526
waccamawjournal.com

The William & Mary Review
William & Mary
P.O. Box 8795
Williamsburg, VA 23187-8795
wm.edu/so/wmreview

Willow Springs
501 N Riverpoint BLVD Ste. 425
Spokane, WA 99201-3903
willowsprings.ewu.edu

*Apple Valley Review: A Journal of
Contemporary Literature*
88 South 3rd Street, Suite 336
San Jose, CA 95113
applevalleyreview.com

Canada

Room
P.O. Box 46160
Station D
Vancouver, BC V6J5G5
roommagazine.com

Participating Writing Programs

MFA Program in Creative Writing
American University
Department of Literature
4400 Massachusetts Avenue N.W.
Washington, DC 20016

University Creative Writing Program
Arizona State
Creative Writing
English Dept.
Tempe, AZ 85287
english.clas.asu.edu/creativewriting

MFA Program in Creative Writing
Brooklyn College
Department of English
2900 Bedford Avenue
Brooklyn, NY 11210

Program in Literary Arts
Brown University
Box 1923
Providence, RI 02912
brown.edu/Departments/Literary_
Arts

Creative Writing Program
Colorado State University
Department of English
359 Eddy Building
Fort Collins, CO 80523-1773

MFA in Creative Writing-Poetry
Columbia College Chicago
600 South Michigan Avenue
Chicago, IL 60660
colum.edu/academics/english_
department/poetry/mfa.php

MFA in Creative Writing
Emerson College
120 Boylston Street
Boston, MA 02116-1596
emerson.edu

Writing Fellowship
Fine Arts Work Center in
Provincetown
24 Pearl Street
Provincetown, MA 02657
fawc.org

MFA Program in Creative Writing
Florida International University
Department of English, Biscayne Bay
Camp
3000 N.E. 151st Street
North Miami, FL 33181

Department of English
Florida State University
Williams Building
Tallahassee, FL 32306-1580
english.fsu.edu/crw/index.html

Creative Writing Program
George Mason University
4400 University Drive
MS 3E4
Fairfax, VA 22030
creativewriting.gmu.edu

Creative Writing Program
Hollins University
P.O. Box 9677
Jackson Center for Creative Writing
at Hollins
Roanoke, VA 24020

MFA Program
Hunter College
68th and Lexington
New York, NY 10065

The Writing Seminars
Johns Hopkins University
081 Gilman Hall
3400 North Charles Street
Baltimore, MD 21218-2690
writingseminars.jhu.edu

Writing Program
Kalamazoo College
English Dept.
1200 Academy St.
Kalamazoo, MI 49006
kzoo.edu/programs/?id=12

Asian American Poetry Retreat
Kundiman
P. O. Box 4248
Sunnyside, NY 11104
kundiman.org

English Department
Louisiana State University
260 Allen
Baton Rouge, LA 70803
english.lsu.edu/dept/programs/
creative_writing

Program in Creative Writing
McNeese State University
P.O. Box 92655
Lake Charles, LA 70609
mfa.mcneese.edu

Creative Writing Program
Minnesota State University, Mankato
230 Armstrong Hall
Mankato, MN 56001
english.mnsu.edu

Department of English
New Mexico State University
Box 30001
Department 3E
Las Cruces, NM 88003-8001
nmsu.edu

Graduate Writing Program
The New School
66 West 12th Street, Room 505
New York, NY 10011

Graduate Program in Creative Writing
New York University
58 W. 10th St
New York, NY 10011

Creative Writing Program
Ohio State University
Department of English, 421 Denney
Hall
164 West 17th Avenue
Columbus, OH 43210-1370
english.osu.edu/programs/
creativewriting/default.cfm

Creative Writing
Ohio University
360 Ellis Hall
Athens, OH 45701
english.ohiou.edu/cw

Master of Fine Arts in Creative
Writing
Pacific University
2043 College Way
Forest Grove, OR 97116
pacificu.edu/as/mfa

MFA in Creative Writing
Pennsylvania State University
Department of English
S. 144 Burrowes Building
University Park, PA 16802

Master of Fine Arts Program
San Diego State University
Department of English and
Comparative Literature
San Diego, CA 92182

Creative Writing Department
San Francisco State University
College of Liberal & Creative Arts
1600 Holloway Avenue
San Francisco, CA 94132-4162

Office of Graduate Studies
Sarah Lawrence College
1 Mead Way
Bronxville, NY 10708-5999

MA in English, Creative Writing
Southeastern Missouri State
MS 2650, English Department
Cape Girardeau, MO 63701

Program in Creative Writing
Syracuse University
Department of English
401 Hall of Languages
Syracuse, NY 13244-1170
english.syr.edu/graduate/mfa.htm

MFA Program in Creative Writing
Texas State University
Department of English
601 University Drive, Flowers Hall
San Marcos, TX 78666
txstate.edu

Creative Writing Program
Texas Tech University
English Department
Lubbock, TX 79409-3091
english.ttu.edu/cw

Creative Writing MFA
University of Massachusetts Boston
Wheatley Building, Floor: 06, Room
00052
100 Morrissey Blvd.
Boston, MA 02125-3393
umb.edu/academics/cla/english/grad/
mfa

Program in Creative Writing
University of Alabama
Department of English
P.O. Box 870244
Tuscaloosa, AL 35487-0244
english.ua.edu/grad/cw

Fairbanks Program in Creative
Writing
University of Alaska
Department of English
P.O. Box 755720
Fairbanks, AK 99775-5720
uaf.edu/english

Creative Writing Program
University of Arizona
Department of English
Modern Languages Bldg. #67
Tucson, AZ 85721-0067
cwp.web.arizona.edu

Program in Creative Writing
University of Arkansas
Department of English
333 Kimpel Hall
Fayetteville, AR 72701
uark.edu/depts/english/PCWT.html

MFA@FLA (Creative Writing
Program)
University of Florida
Department of English
P.O. Box 11730
Gainesville, FL 32611-7310
english.ufl.edu/crw

Creative Writing Program
University of Hawaii
English Department
1733 Donaghho Road
Honolulu, HI 96822
english.hawaii.edu/cw

Creative Writing Program
University of Houston
Department of English
R. Cullen 229
Houston, TX 77204-3015

Creative Writing Program
University of Idaho
Department of English
Moscow, ID 83843-1102
class.uidaho.edu/english/CW/
mfaprogram.html

Program for Writers
University of Illinois at Chicago
Department of English MC/162
601 South Morgan Street
Chicago, IL 60607-7120
uic.edu/depts/engl

Program in Creative Writing
University of Iowa
102 Dey House
507 North Clinton Street
Iowa City, IA 52242

University of Kansas MFA Program
Wescoe Hall
Lawrence, KS 66405
www2.ku.edu/~englishmfa

Creative Writing Program
University of Maryland
Department of English
3119F Susquehanna Hall
College Park, MD 20742
english.umd.edu/programs/
CreateWriting/index.html

MFA Program for Poets and Writers
University of Massachusetts
452 Bartlett Hall
130 Hicks Way
Amherst, MA 01003-9269
umass.edu/english/eng/mfa

Master of Fine Arts in English
University of Mississippi
Bondurant Hall C135
P. O. Box 1848
University, MS 38677-1848
olemiss.edu/depts/english/mfa/home.
htm

Master of Fine Arts in Creative
Writing Program
University of Missouri-St. Louis
Department of English
8001 Natural Bridge Road
St. Louis, MO 63121
umsl.edu/~mfa

MFA Writing Program
University of North Carolina,
Greensboro
3302 MHRA Building
P.O. Box 26170
Greensboro, NC 27402-6170
mfagreensboro.org

Department of English
University of North Texas
1155 Union Circle #311307
Denton, TX 76203-5017
engl.unt.edu/grad/grad_creative.htm

Creative Writing Program
University of Notre Dame
356 O'Shaughnessy Hall
Notre Dame, IN 46556-0368
english.nd.edu/creative-writing

MFA in Writing Program
University of San Francisco
Program Office, Kalmanovitz Hall
302
2130 Fulton Street
San Francisco, CA 94117-1080
usfca.edu/artsci/writ

MFA Program
University of South Carolina
Department of English/ MFA
program
University of South Carolina
Columbia, SC 29208
cas.sc.edu/engl/grad/mfa/index.html

Graduate Program Creative Writing
University of South Florida
Department of English, CPR 107
4202 E. Fowler Avenue
Tampa, FL 33620
english.usf.edu/graduate/
concentrations/cw/degrees/

The Center for Writers
The University of Southern
Mississippi
118 College Drive #5144
Hattiesburg, MS 39406
centerforwriters.com

Michener Center for Writers
University of Texas
J. Frank Dobie House
702 East Dean Keeton Street
Austin, TX 78705
utexas.edu/academic/mcw

Creative Writing Program
University of Texas at Austin
1 University Station B5000
English Department
Austin, TX 78712

Creative Writing Program
University of Utah
255 South Central Campus Drive
Room 3500
Salt Lake City, UT 84112

Creative Writing Program
University of Washington
Box 354330
Seattle, WA 98195-4330
University of Washington Creative
Writing

Creative Writing Program
University of Wisconsin-Milwaukee
Department of English
Box 413
Milwaukee, WI 53201

Creative Writing Program
University of Wyoming
P.O. Box 3353
Laramie, WY 82071-2000
uwyo.edu/creativewriting

Unterberg Poetry Center/Writing
Program
92nd Street Y
1395 Lexington Avenue
New York, NY 10128
92Y.org/WritingProgram

MFA in Creative Writing Program
Virginia Commonwealth University
Department of English
P.O. Box 842005
Richmond, VA 23284-2005

MFA Program
Virginia Tech
323 Shanks Hall
English Department, Virginia Tech
Blacksburg, VA 24061
english.vt.edu/graduate/MFA/index.
html

Creative Writing Program
Wayne State University
English Department, 5057 Woodward
Ave., 9th floor
Detroit, MI 48202

Creative Writing Program
West Virginia University
Department of English
P.O. Box 6296
Morgantown, WV 26506-6296
as.wvu.edu/english

MFA in Creative and Professional
Writing
Western Connecticut State University
181 White St.
Danbury, CT 06810
wcsu.edu/writing/mfa

Whidbey Writers Workshop
P.O. Box 639
Freeland, WA 98249
writeonwhidbey.org/mfa

Canada

Creative Writing Program
University of British Columbia
Buchanan E462-1866 Main Mall
Vancouver, BC V6T 1Z1
creativewriting.ubc.ca

MATTHEW DICKMAN is the author of *Mayakovsky's Revolver* (W.W. Norton, 2012), *All-American Poem* (American Poetry Review, 2008), winner of the May Sarton Award from the American Academy of Arts and Sciences, and co-author with Michael Dickman of *50 American Plays* (Copper Canyon, 2012). He has received the Kate Tufts Discovery Award, as well as residencies and fellowships from the Provincetown Fine Arts Work Center, the Vermont Studio Center, Literary Arts of Oregon, and the Lannan Foundation. He lives in Portland, Oregon.

JAZZY DANZIGER is the author of *Darkroom* (University of Wisconsin, 2012), winner of the Brittingham Prize in Poetry. She lives in St. Louis, Missouri and can be visited online at jazzydanziger.com.